A Guide to Creating a Successful Algorithmic Trading Strategy

A Guide to Creating a Successful Algorithmic Trading Strategy

PERRY J. KAUFMAN

WILEY

For general information on our other products and services or for technical support,
please contact our Customer Care Department within the United States at (800)
762-2974, outside the United States at (317) 572-3993, or fax (317) 572-4002.

Wiley publishes in a variety of print and electronic formats and by print-on-demand.
Some material included with standard print versions of this book may not be
included in e-books or in print-on-demand. If this book refers to media such as a
CD or DVD that is not included in the version you purchased, you may download
this material at http://booksupport.wiley.com. For more information about Wiley
products, visit www.wiley.com.

ISBN 978-1-119-22474-7 (Hardcover)
ISBN 978-1-119-22476-1 (ePDF)
ISBN 978-1-11-9-22475-4 (ePub)

Printed in the United States of America.
10 9 8 7 6 5 4 3 2 1

Contents

Acknowledgments

My special thanks to three people with incredible knowledge in this area, and who could have easily written this themselves, John Kowalik, John Ehlers, and Linda Raschke. They generously provided very extensive and insightful comments that resulted in numerous changes and hopefully, considerably more clarity. My appreciation also goes to Mark Rzepczynski, who tenaciously questioned some of my conclusions and to Ernie Varitimos and Murray Ruggiero for their insight.

To my mother, Helen, who has proofread every book that I've written. If you find any errors, please direct your comments to her.

Thank you all.

PJK

* * *

A reminder from Barbara Rockefeller's Morning Forex Briefing:

The researches of many commentators have already thrown much darkness on this subject, and it is probable that if they continue we shall soon know nothing at all.

—*Mark Twain*

CHAPTER 1

A Brief Introduction: The Ground Rules

Everything should be made as simple as possible, but not simpler.

—Albert Einstein

If you haven't heard it, a classic example of trading experience is the difference between a statistician and a trader. You flip a coin 99 times and it comes up heads each time. You ask the statistician, "What are the odds that it will come up heads next time?" The statistician answers, "50:50." You ask the trader the same question and he answers, "100 percent." Surprised, you ask the trader, "Why?" He responds, "Because it couldn't possibly be a fair coin. The odds of getting 99 heads in a row are too high to have happened by chance." Experience transforms theory into reality.

When I first started trading using automated systems in the early 1970s, the very idea was demeaned by professional traders as "ridiculous," "the market just doesn't work that way," "you can't make money if you don't know the value of the stock." Now that opinion seems to have been turned upside down. High frequency trading, the algorithmic trading system on steroids, has "an unfair advantage," "it's stealing money from the ordinary investor." Times have changed, but attitudes have not.

MY OBJECTIVE

This is a no-frills book. It's short because it just deals with the most important issues of developing a successful trading system and because you're more likely to read it all. It is intended to be a painless lesson in reality, those critical steps that you learn over time, often by doing them wrong. For some, it will be a confirmation that you're getting it right, and for others it may be an "Aha!" moment. It would be more responsible, and more scientific, to verify each of my conclusions yourself. But, if you're like me, you readily accept ideas that are reasonable and seem right, and you choose to believe them. I've been uncertain at times, but I rarely regret a decision that comes from common sense.

Each chapter contains, in my opinion, the best way to deal with the various aspects of creating a trading system. All of the steps are important, and doing them incorrectly will show up later in your trading account, perhaps too late. It's better to spend a little extra time up front to increase your chances of success later on.

THE GROUND RULES

Before we get immersed in the details, there are some important items to define and disclose.

First, we all have biases. They are often found in what we don't say rather than what we actually state. I see that when I watch the political commentary on television and also in the evening news. Everyone seems to have an agenda.

My own biases are toward fully automatic trading, which include all the good and bad of it. I also like macrotrend systems, stock and various other arbitrage, and some pattern recognition, among other methods that I can't remember right now. I don't like systems with a lot of rules and I'm suspicious of systems that work on only one market. I'm going to try to balance my examples to show short-term and long-term systems, but the reality is that there will probably be more about long-term trend following, which I believe is used by more traders, especially at the early stages when they are dangling their collective toes in the water.

THE PROCESS

The process of developing a trading strategy involves eight well-defined steps, shown in Figure 1.1. These should be clear, except for the marks on the left that show "Change rules" and "Failed." From the top down, the trading idea comes first, then you need to get all the data that will be used to validate your strategy. You must have a trading platform to test your idea, which could be as simple as Excel, or as sophisticated as TradeStation. You enter your rules using that platform.

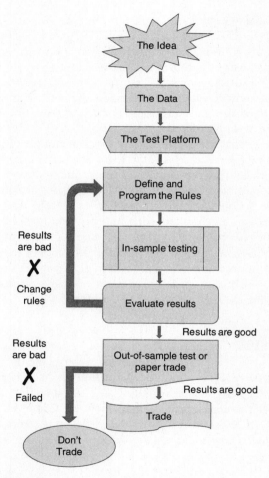

FIGURE 1.1 The Development Process

You begin testing using in-sample data (more about this in Chapters 10 and 11) and evaluate the results. If they are not what you want, go back and change the rules, then retest them using the in-sample data. Continue to do this until you're satisfied with the results. Then test the strategy on out-of-sample data, which you've held aside and not used. If it works, and we'll explain what "works" means later, you're ready to trade.

However, it doesn't usually unfold that smoothly. When you use the out-of-sample data, the results are not as good as you expected. So you go back and change the rules. But now you no longer have the out-of-sample data that are needed to verify your work. Purists would say that, once you fail the out-of-sample test, then you need to discard the system and start with something new. But that never actually happens. We're sure that the method still works, but we've overlooked something that now seems obvious, such as using volatility instead of fixed values for placing the stop-loss. Or, we should have added profit-taking.

There is a way out. When you're all done testing and the results finally look good, you can paper trade. That way, you track the results with no money and see if they are close to your expectations. The problem is that it takes time and we're usually impatient to make money—or in some cases, to lose money. Experience says that there are probably still changes to be made, so paper trading is your punishment for looking at the out-of-sample data more than once.

BASIC TRADING SYSTEMS

We'll be using both trend-following and short-term systems as examples throughout this book, so a brief definition should be helpful.

The Trend System

A trend is most easily defined by a new high or a new low price, but a moving average is more common, so we'll use a moving average as an example most often. There is some discussion of the difference between trending methods, primarily in Chapter 3. We'll explain the most important features of a few different methods, but the differences aren't as important as the way the trend concept works.

For a moving average system, we'll define the buy-and-sell signals when the trend turns up and down, and not when the price penetrates the trendline. Once you have accepted the concept that the trendline gives you the trend direction (not a difficult concept to embrace), the trendline is the only important value. You can ignore the price for the purpose of generating buy-and-sell signals.

Short-Term Systems

While trend systems are mostly similar, short-term systems can be very different. Examples will focus on their common properties, such as volatility, risk, and costs, as well as frequently used rules, such as profit-taking and stops.

Short-term trading systems can be more complex than trend following. We'll discuss a number of pattern-based approaches as well as intraday breakouts.

With this brief background, let's jump into the development of an algorithmic trading strategy.

CHAPTER 2

The Idea

Where do you get trading ideas? They're everywhere, but they require your intuitive sense to recognize, and they must be easy to explain. You can't find a successful trading system by combining indicators, time periods, patterns, and other techniques in a computer. You will find something that worked brilliantly in the past, but with little hope of it working in the future.

BEGIN AT THE BEGINNING

You must start with a sound premise. That could be:

- Trends based on interest rate policy set by the Fed.
- Seasonal patterns that exist in agriculture, airline stocks, vacation resorts, heating oil, and other stocks and commodities.
- Exploiting the difference between two similar stocks, such as two chip manufacturers, pharmaceutical companies, or home builders. That's called *stock arbitrage*, or pairs trading.

- Buying or selling price volatility before an earnings report or after a price shock.
- Fading an upgrade announcement by a major firm (old news by the time it prints on the screen).
- Same-time-next-month patterns, when funds redeem and add to their positions.
- The 3-day cycle, based on human nature, but dependable for 50 years.
- Weekly patterns, such as, "Up on Monday, down on Tuesday."

There are many others, but to recognize these opportunities you must trade. Trading is the best way to concentrate your attention on the market and absorb the effects (on your money) of economic reports, geopolitical events, and specific company news. With money in the market, your focus on price movement is greatly increased and you look to quickly resolve the problems that cause losses.

You can also read books on trading, listen to webinars, and attend lectures given by notable gurus. Many of these will provide good ideas, but none will give you a trading system you can start using today. Mostly, they will provide important knowledge "in the margin." That is, you might learn how to size a position or where to place a stop, but it is unlikely that anyone is going to hand you his or her best trading method, even if you're paying big bucks to attend his or her session. You still have to learn the art of trading yourself.

THE IDEA MUST MATCH YOUR TRADING PERSONALITY

So it's up to you to find a sound idea that is compatible with your way of trading—your trading personality. Some investors can put on a position and hold it for a year, others are out the moment the price goes the wrong way. Don't force yourself to trade in a way that bothers you.

My wife and I are both traders, so in our house we talk markets every day. This can be frustrating for both of us because we have very different trading styles. For many years, she was an exchange member and floor trader. Operating as a traditional market-maker, she went long or short during the day, ending the day (usually) flat. For her, holding a trade for a long time means taking a position home overnight. Our opinion of market direction is often different because of our time frame. She will say, "The market is crashing!" and I'll look at a 3-point drop in the S&P over the past two hours and say, "Where?" She still favors the short side because money is made faster and floor traders prefer to take the opposite side of the retail investor.

Not long after the 2008 financial crisis, we agreed (not a small achievement) that the battered market must certainly be offering a lifetime opportunity. We decided to diversify among sectors and take long-term positions in good companies representing energy, health care, and a few other areas we thought had sustained potential. Decisions were made and she set the positions.

The next week, four or five days after she allocated the assets, she came into my office with a Cheshire cat grin, saying, "We're out and we made a very good profit."—"Great." I must have been mistaken about holding those positions for a year.

The lesson here is that it's difficult to change your trading personality. If you're a short-term trader, then find a short-term strategy. If you don't like to look at the market every day, then use long-term trend following, even weekly signals, and just monitor the results weekly. Don't fight your nature. You'll lose.

I NEED A FAST PAYOUT

Some people start trading in hopes of generating income quickly. I know of one man who has $50,000 to invest and "needs" to draw $2,500 each month to live. To retain the same principal, he would need to earn a 50% return each year, which is very unrealistic. The more likely scenario is that drawing out funds will cause the account to slowly dwindle away until there is nothing left to trade.

Even if you have more patience to let profits accumulate, be aware that slower trading systems, ones that hold positions for weeks, will have larger equity swings and a lower percentage of profitable trades. Even fast systems can have sequences of losses amounting to the same drawdown. The more risk you take, the larger the drawdowns. Even thinking that you can withdraw profits by the end of a year is unrealistic. Not all years produce profits, even when the trading system is good. You might be in a natural equity downturn, which is a bad time to take money out. You'll need to view your trading capital as a long-term investment for you to reap the benefits.

WITHSTANDING THE TEST OF TIME

The ideas for strategies listed at the beginning of this Chapter are those that have withstood the test of time. Perhaps with only small changes. There are some traders who want their system to have shown profits for at least 15 years. There are others who are willing to say, "If it's worked for the past three years and it's still making the same profits, it's worth trading."

Long-term trend following has continued to be profitable for 30 years, and pairs trading is a concept that will always work. These two, among others, may not be as profitable now because of more competition, but they still work. That can be reassuring as well as a good starting point.

Then there are systems that need to be "adjusted" from time to time. For example, I had a fund during the 1990s that traded a short-term intraday breakout. Granted, the 1990s was a good period, especially for interest rate futures, which only went up. But as we got to 1997 and yields were lower, along with volatility, the daily profits got much smaller. If the markets that were contributing most of the profits no longer produced as much, the performance of the fund would suffer badly.

The rules of the system were to buy or sell a breakout after an opening range was established, then hold the trade overnight and exit on the open the next day. The trade could only be held overnight, a total of one day. The solution was simple. Allow the trade to be held until the new trade signal occurred. If it was in the same direction as the current position, we held the old trade. If not, we reversed. That increased the returns per trade, and also the risk, but the returns were now large enough to offset other losses. A small change that did not alter the concept, but resulted in the necessary improvement. From time to time, changes may be needed.

Then there are strategies that take advantage of temporary market patterns. We used to see crude oil close strong every day during the early 2000s. It looked as though a large trader was buying every day on the close. We started to buy 10 minutes before the close and did well for about a month. Then it stopped. After a few days of nothing happening, we abandoned the strategy, but had netted a nice profit.

There are an unlimited number of strategies that can be profitable, as long as you are observant and are willing to take the risk.

CHAPTER 3

Don't Make It Complex

We all know the phrase "Keep it simple, stupid." It's true. Making a system gratuitously complex is self-defeating. Complexity is not sophisticated; it's just confusing. When there are too many moving parts, you can lose track of what is working and what is not. It's difficult to understand something complex and it's difficult to fix when it goes wrong, which is very likely to happen. In Chapter 2, we said that the idea needed to be easily understood. Try to keep it that way as you develop your idea into a trading system.

One phrase that was used by a well-known fund manager is, "Loose pants fit everyone." I believe that. I want my trading method to work in as many different markets as possible, and the more rules there are, the less likely that will happen. The problem is that "loose pants" look awful. In trading, it means that you will take bigger risks, have longer periods of losses, and always feel that you could have avoided some ugly move by adding another rule. That's not really true. Losses, some of them large, will occur anyway. We'll discuss this in Chapter 13.

A trading method that works over a long period of time and in many markets is "robust." I like robust. It means that there is something fundamentally correct about the strategy. For example, some years ago the "Intraday Break-out System" was the rage. The process was:

- Record the high and low of the first hour of trading.
- Buy a new high or sell a new low after the first hour.
- You can exit at the end of the day but it was better to hold the trade into the next day and apply the same rules.

That's actually only one rule (I always allow for a symmetric buy-and-sell signal), and it worked on many stocks and futures markets for years. It doesn't do as well now because some markets have changed and other traders have worked out similar approaches, but it still generates profits in markets that have an underlying trend. In case you're wondering, it won't work on the equity index markets because they have too much noise, *noise* being erratic, less predictable price changes from day to day. Traders in interest rates, FX, and many stocks continue to use it.

Pairs trading also works. You find two stocks in a similar business, such as microchips, or driven by much the same dynamics, such as disposable income, and, when they move apart, you sell the more expensive one and buy the cheaper one. As with trend following, the competition has increased and the profits have gotten smaller. But there are still opportunities for profiting using strategies that are easy to understand and fundamentally sound.

Simple trading methods aren't hard to find; they're just not perfect and their equity curves are never as smooth as you want them to be. As long as it has a sound concept, you need to recognize and accept its flaws.

A WORD ABOUT NOISE

It's very likely that I see price noise as more important than others, so I'll take a minute to explain why. In the 1970s, I developed the *efficiency ratio*, a way of measuring how smoothly prices moved. It is the ratio of the difference between the first and last price (over *n* days), divided by the sum of the individual day's moves, all values taken as a positive number. Think about it in terms of a drunken sailor's walk.

When a sailor leaves his ship he's sober. He walks straight to the nearest pub in the fewest steps possible. That's 100% efficient. On his way back, he's not so steady and he staggers up one alley and down the next, eventually finding his way back to the ship. If we take the first path to the pub, divided by the distance of the return path, we find the efficiency of his return path. The more he drinks, the less efficient he is.

What does it mean when we measure price movement in the same way? My interpretation is that a highly efficient price move can be exploited using any simple trend strategy. A very noisy price move is ideal for mean reversion. If we study all the futures markets, we find that the highest noise is in the most mature markets, the S&P and NASDAQ, followed by the European index markets. The ones with the least noise are the short-term interest rates, such as Eurodollars and short sterling, and also the emerging country equity index markets.

I tend to be skeptical of systems that trade in conflict to this idea, that is, attempt to extract mean reversion profits from the Euribor, or expect large gains from a macrotrend system tracking the S&P.

INTEGRATED SOLUTIONS VERSUS BUILDING BLOCKS

What good is a computer if you can't throw in everything you know and get out the best solution? That's certainly how many new traders think. Even with experience, the temptation is to let the computer do the work so we don't need to do the hard thinking. The perfect tools for doing it wrong are genetic algorithms, neural networks, and optimization. Of course they are valuable tools, but they are grossly abused. We're going to ignore the heavy math and talk about optimization later, and explain why these can lead you down the wrong path.

There are two popular approaches when it comes to building a trading strategy:

1. Define each rule and test them one at a time, independent of other rules.
2. Put all the rules into the blender at the same time and test them to capture the interaction.

Consider the first approach. Define each rule and test it individually to see if that rule is profitable and if it improves the basic strategy. Suppose we have developed a trend system and want to add profit-taking and a high-volatility filter. First, we would test various levels for taking profits to see if that improved the results of our basic trend test. Next, we would void the profit-taking and test the high-volatility filter by blocking entries when the historical price volatility was above, say 50%. We would then compare the filtered results with the original test to see if there was an improvement. We would not do the two tests at the same time. In this approach, each rule is a building block that must stand on its own before it is used.

We can test both profit-taking and high volatility at the same time for a fully integrated solution. This is possible only because computer processing power continues to improve. The thought is that these two features might interact in a way that results in a better selection of parameter values. For example, we might want the volatility filter at 60% or 70% instead of a lower threshold, because the profit-taking rule was able to capture profits when the volatility was at 55%.

I'm a supporter of building blocks. I like to know that each feature works. It bothers me if one feature actually loses money on its own, but is profitable in combination with another rule. Of course it's possible. I just don't like it.

If we carry this to an extreme, we could have 10 rules working together, ultimately producing a profit greater than the combination found tested separately. It's a truly integrated solution. But what if performance starts to deteriorate? Which of the 10 rules is a problem? If you change one rule, then others are likely to be affected. It becomes too complicated and difficult to sort out and unwind, much like the 2008 financial crisis. Because each of the building blocks is easy to understand, and each stands on its own, I stay with that approach.

MORE RULES, FEWER OPPORTUNITIES, LESS SUCCESS

We should all know about *overfitting*. It's when you fine-tune your strategy, using rules and specific parameters so it works brilliantly. At least it works on historical data. As a rule, the more parameters in a strategy, the fewer opportunities are found, and the less likely it will work over time. The quants call it "too many degrees of freedom," in which a lot of parameters lead to overfitting. I think of it as an octopus with too many legs. You are able to capture events in the past by molding the rules to fit the situations. For that to work in the future, the new events must unfold in nearly the same way as they did in the past. That's hardly likely.

Our government has tried to regulate the financial industry to avoid "too big to fail," giving mortgages to people with no income, piggy-backing orders that could cause a "flash crash," and essentially trying to fix all the problems of the past. That's how governments work. If they regulated everything in advance, we wouldn't be able to do anything.

The problem is that risk is like the children's game Whack-A-Mole. A mole pops up out of a hole and you smash it down with a mallet, only to see another pop up somewhere else. It's the same with the market. No matter what we do to stop it, there will always be crashes, price shocks, and unexpected crises popping up. It's the nature of the market. While the government is trying to smash them down, we need to figure out how to reduce their impact. We'll discuss this under the sections specifically focused on risk.

CHAPTER 4

Why Should I Care about "Robust" If I'm Trading Only Apple?

Why indeed? There are traders who are certainly specialists in different stocks. They know the company, the balance sheets, the business plan, and assess the skill of management. They try to buy when the stock is relatively undervalued and they see long-term potential. Some of these traders make money at it, some make lots of money, and others lose. Some make money because they are fundamentally right, but it takes a year or two before they see profits. We don't really know how many are successful, but we do know what makes a successful systematic trader: a robust system and the discipline to follow it.

The idea behind robustness is that it must work over different markets and different time periods, using the same rules. It's a way of making sure that a strategy isn't fine-tuned to the specific ups and downs of one stock or futures market. As you might have figured out by now, a robust system will have only a few rules.

IS IT ROBUST?

How do you know if it's robust? Let's start with the idea behind my old friend, the trend. Trends track fundamentals, such as interest rate policy or supply and demand imbalances. In my experience, they need to be slow to successfully recognize economic trends, in the range of 60 to 250 days. A faster tracking period, of about 30 to 100 days, is needed for seasonality or supply-and-demand imbalances. So, if we test every trend in the slow range on the SPY, and all of them are profitable (net of costs), then we can clearly say that the strategy is robust. But wait. Now let's try it on the QQQ, the IWM, and some futures markets, such as the 10-year note and crude oil. Voilà! They are all profitable. Now we have verified that a system works over varying time periods and in different markets. Yes, my students, it is robust.

Unfortunately, very few strategies are so robust that they are profitable in every time frame and every market. If 70% of your tests were profitable, it should be considered a great success. Long-term trend following is one of those systems that is robust, which is why so many professional managers use long-term trends as all or part of their trading portfolio. Stock arbitrage is also robust but less liquid and more trading intense.

The two charts that follow show the returns of a moving average system using a range of calculation periods from 10 to 200 days. The only trading rule is that we calculate the moving average, then enter a position in the direction of the trend of the moving average. Figure 4.1 shows the SPY and Apple (AAPL) net profits (long only), and Figure 4.2 shows the Eurodollar interest rates (ED, both long and short positions). Eurodollars are the price of the 3-month maturity on U.S. dollars deposited abroad (note the yield is 100 minus

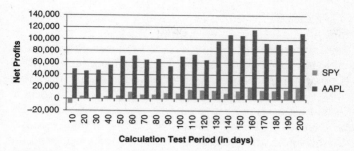

FIGURE 4.1 SPY and AAPL Moving Average Optimization Net Profits

the price). The net profits are on the left scale and the moving average calculation period, from 10 to 200 days, on the bottom. The data started at 1990 or the earliest available. Costs were $8 per stock transaction and $8 per contract per side for futures. The position size for the SPY test is a $10,000 investment divided by the closing price. For ED, it is a $25,000 investment divided by the 20-day volatility, using the average true range, expressed in dollars.

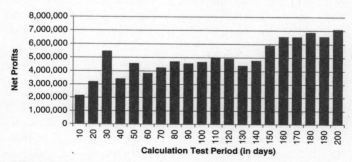

FIGURE 4.2 ED Interest Rates Moving Average Optimization

With one exception, the 10-day moving average of SPY, all the tests were profitable. That's pretty impressive. Pay attention to the pattern of performance in both charts.

There are two traps here. The first is that you need to define the time horizon and the markets in advance. You need a concept that says, "If this system works, then it should work on most interest rates and the major FX markets, and it should work using longer calculation periods." Not all stocks and futures markets perform as well as these, but you will find that a high percentage will be profitable.

I like to use the range 40 to 120 for trend following. That would have missed the best returns of Apple and SPY, as well as some good performance in futures, but they would still have been highly profitable and consistent. It simply reflects my idea of the range of calculation periods in which trends really exist. You may decide differently, as long as you do it before you start testing.

Think about testing 100 different markets with your own strategy. When you look at the results, 50 of them were profitable. Of those 50, five were very profitable. Do you choose one of those five? No, because the best are likely to be successful strictly by chance. That is, they were lucky to be on the right side of some surprise move. You can't count on that happening again. That's why you need to have a much larger percentage of successful tests to be comfortable with the results.

The second trap is the distribution of the tests. It looks as though we're very safe trading any of these markets with a moving average of at least 120 days, but that's an illusion. The results of a 10-day and 15-day moving average can be very different, but the difference between a 190- and 200-day moving average is very small. The result is deceptive. We'll look at this again in Chapter 10.

ANOTHER DIMENSION

There is another dimension to robustness. When you look at a sequence of tests, such as Figures 4.1 and 4.2, the net results should show a smooth transition as the parameter values get larger or smaller. You don't want to see a large gain followed by a loss, followed by another large gain, as in Figure 4.3.

For example, if we're looking for the optimal profit-taking level based on volatility, we calculate the 20-day average true range and multiply that by a factor, and add that value to our entry price to get our long-side profit target. Note that the *true range* is similar to the daily

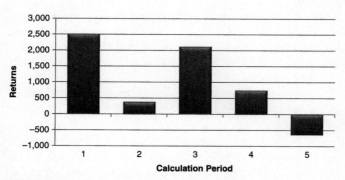

FIGURE 4.3 Inconsistent Results from Optimization

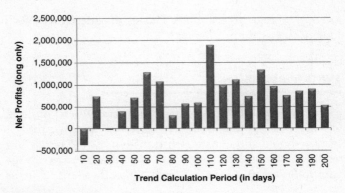

FIGURE 4.4 S&P Futures from 1990, Net Profits by Calculation Period

high-low range but includes the previous closing price if there was a gap opening. We can test the factor from, say, 1.00 to 10.00, that is, from 1 ATR (*average true range*, usually taken over 20 days) to 10 ATRs. We don't expect to get any profit-taking at 10 ATRs, but we need to see the pattern of profits over a wide range. We test the S&P futures from 1990, charging $16 per contract for each round-turn trade.

In Figure 4.4, we see that profits peak at a calculation period of 110. There are some losses at the far left where the cost of trading overwhelms the small profits per trade. Choosing the best results, a 110-day trend, we then apply profit-taking, shown in Figure 4.5. Our goal is to beat the result of the best test. All the results that peak over the $2,000,000 net profit succeed.

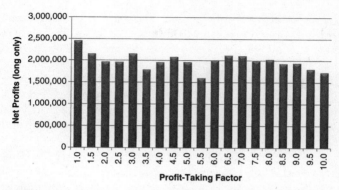

FIGURE 4.5 S&P Futures Net Profits Using Profit-Taking

The results show that profit-taking is best taken quickly, even though costs are a bigger factor. There is an erratic pattern in the middle, which smooths out to the right and then declines as fewer profits are taken. While this is only one example, it is typical of test results. There is a pattern but it is never perfectly smooth. It is always smoother toward the right, where the percentage differences in the parameters get smaller and there are fewer trades. Visualizing the results allows you to make a better choice. It's all about consistency.

BUT WHICH PARAMETER VALUE DO I TRADE?

The next problem is, "Which trend speed do I pick?" If I have 70 of 100 (or fewer) that are successful, how do I decide which to use? Most people would pick the one with the highest profit, or the best reward for risk, or the smallest drawdown. That would be a mistake. The highest profit might be the system with the moving average just fast enough to get short before a meltdown, or exit before a price shock. It will be the one best tuned to the stock you're testing and its specific pattern *in the past*. But the past is not the future. It's the most likely to underperform your expectations next year. Then, do you pick the worst and expect it to outperform? No, not that either.

We can't really know which parameters will be best next year. The problem is the same as picking stocks in a portfolio. If you pick only one, you might have the highest return or the biggest loss. If you pick two, you reduce the possibility of the largest return, but you also reduce the risk, and you gain stability. So you do the same selecting parameters and rules as you would to get diversification—you trade more than one set of parameters. In doing that, you give up the best results but you also mitigate the worst.

MULTIPLE TIME FRAMES

By *multiple time frames*, I mean different calculation periods. The solution is to pick at least four combinations and treat them equally, that is, trade the same amount on each choice. It is worth repeating that if you put more money (more risk) on any one system or stock, it must outperform all others or you're just adding risk.

For the aspiring quants, be sure that when testing or selecting parameters, you use a nonlinear distribution. A *linear distribution* would be moving averages from 10 to 100, in steps of 5. But the difference between a 10- and a 15-day moving average is very large, and the difference between 95 and 100 days is small. If you test equal intervals and average the results, you are heavily weighting the larger calculation periods (slower trends). Using a nonlinear distribution means that each next parameter value is a multiple of the previous one (a percentage change), so that you get the new test values 20, 30, 45, 67.5, 101.25, by multiplying the previous value by 1.5 (and then rounding to a whole number).

In many of the systems that I've created and traded, a simple choice is to use 30-, 60-, and 120-day periods. That covers the range and is distributed correctly so it doesn't give more weight to either the long-term or short-term systems.

IS ONE TREND METHOD BETTER THAN ANOTHER?

Experience has shown me that all trend methods work when markets trend and all of them fail when markets don't trend. It's not the method of finding the trend, it's the market. There are differences in the internal profiles of each trend strategy. For example, moving averages have a lot of small losses and a low percentage of good trades. A breakout system has a much higher percentage of good trades, but holds large losses to achieve that. Every trader must decide which profile is most comfortable for him or her.

Personally, I like breakout systems because the actual point of breakout (a new high or low) means that something new has happened. It seems timelier to me. I also don't believe that a stock or futures market must go steadily in one direction, even when it's in a trend. A breakout system gives prices a lot of latitude to wiggle around, the difference between the *n*-day high and the *n*-day low. A moving average keeps advancing steadily upward, even when prices start going sideways. It can get you out of the trade even when prices haven't really reversed.

To show the difference in performance, Figures 4.6 and 4.7 show net profits, over the same range of calculation periods, for the U.S. 30-year bond and crude oil, using moving average (MA), breakout (BO), and linear regression slope (LRS) systems. The rules are:

- The MA system goes long when the moving average turns up and short when it turns down.
- The BO system goes long when there is a new high and short when there is a new low.
- The LRS system goes long when the slope turns positive and short when the slope turns negative.

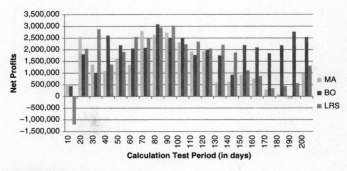

FIGURE 4.6 U.S. Bond Optimization

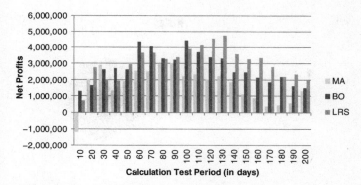

FIGURE 4.7 Crude Oil Optimization Using a Moving Average (MA), Breakout (BO), and Linear Regression Slope (LRS)

Both charts show a similar pattern of performance, with the peak performance about center left and lower returns on both ends. There are only two tests that posted losses.

For bonds, which have had a very long bull market, results vary between systems for the faster calculation periods. They are about the same in the middle, and the breakout is best at the right. We won't try to analyze why. Crude oil is much more uniform and it is difficult to see which trend method works best without more detail.

What I take away from this is that the three trending methods could all net about the same, even though each has a very different risk profile. To decide which is best for you, you will need to create and review the performance yourself. It's more detail than we want to discuss here. The big picture is that trend following is popular because many variations work. When combined with other short-term strategies, it can add stability to your portfolio.

CHAPTER **5**

Less Is More

Trend following aside, there are significant advantages to short-term trading. Being in the market less often can have important advantages.

Short-term trading can produce a much smoother equity stream than trend following. If you're a long-term trend trader, you will suffer the big drawdowns even though the trend is intact. To hold on to the trade, you go through some nasty losses. Just to add more frustration, the end of a trend that is held for a long time is expected to give up 10% to 20% of the gains, sometimes more.

Most short-term trading will have a high percentage of profitable trades. The normal profile, whether you are looking for fast breakouts or fading the price move (mean reversion), is that both profits and losses should be small, and profits should be much more frequent, perhaps more than 70% of the trades. There's no built-in expectation that you'll give back a huge amount of your gains, so it's possible to have a long, smooth, profitable period.

There is another, even more interesting benefit of short-term trading. If your strategy is in the market only 15% of the trading days, then you've avoided 85% of the price shocks. Just to be clear, a *price shock* is a large, violent, often unpleasant price move. It's no small advantage to avoid a price shock. We can't predict a price shock and some of them can wipe you out, so not being in the market is the only realistic way of avoiding them.

If you can make enough profit with less exposure to daily uncertainty, you're all the better for it.

VOLATILITY CUTS BOTH WAYS

You may think this is all hindsight, and to a great degree, it is, but we learn from our experiences. Some of those experiences are one-offs and others can be a valuable lesson for the future.

In 2008, we suffered a crisis that caused all markets to reverse, mostly to the downside. Those moves were violent and sustained. If we use the standard 20-day calculation for annualized volatility, the same used for options, we find that SPY volatility nearly touched 100% (see Figure 5.1). Of course, no one would pay the full cash price of a stock as the option premium. It's just that using only 20 days in the calculation and extrapolating it to a full year causes an unrealistic distortion. But it does show the relative volatility, and 2008 was clearly extreme.

Many systematic traders think that high volatility translates into high profits. That used to be true, and it may still translate into some profits, but at what cost? When the industry was young, we looked only at profits, never at risk. Who cares about risk when you're making so much money? But that's not true in today's noisy and competitive environment.

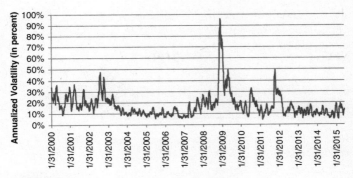

FIGURE 5.1 SPY Annualized Volatility (in Percent)

Smart investors want good returns relative to their risk. So do I. It turns out that during high volatility periods you can net a profit, but the risk in doing that is very high, too high to be a good trade.

Is that overfitting? It's true that I've looked at past volatility to decide the best place, in terms of volatility, to get out of a trade, or not enter a new trade. But does it make sense for the future? I think so because it solves a fundamental problem. When volatility is high, there is always more risk. When volatility is very high, there is very high risk. If one of those trades is not profitable, then you own the risk. It can be a big loss whether you're trading your own money or a client's, and it will be a black spot on your performance that can't be erased.

Be more conservative. There are plenty of trades. Don't take the ones that can really hurt. You can identify them automatically by using the formula for annualized volatility.

For my own systems, when volatility moves over 50%, I get out. Some systems get out as low as 40%. We'll look at this again in Chapter 11.

BULL MARKETS HAPPEN WHEN EVERYONE IS IN DENIAL

It may seem counterintuitive, but as long as the general public is uncertain why the market is rising, or expects it to go down, or the economic numbers are confusing, prices will continue to rise. Consider the rally that followed the final decline in 2009 and is, more or less, continuing now, in 2015. At the beginning of the bull market, investors were uncertain whether it was really the bottom. They tended to believe the commentary that said, "This is a false rally. We'll see prices test the bottom again." That didn't happen. But as our economy was strengthening, Europe was having its problems. Portugal, Ireland, Spain, Italy, and the now-infamous Greece were all in despair. For more than a year, the word "contagion" headed every conversation. If one country fails, or pulls out of the European Union, will everyone else follow? Oh, my!

But that hasn't happened and it's taken second row to when the Fed will raise rates and how that will affect the economy. Analysts have said that higher rates can only be bad news. And now the U.S. dollar is very strong. That means exports will suffer. There seems to be no end to bad news, yet the stock market keeps going up.

There are always answers that seem intelligent after the fact, and offer the illusion of understanding, so I'll submit my own. The market is going up because our economy ranks among the strongest in the world. It is also going up because foreign investors are buying U.S. dollars and putting that money into both the stock market and U.S.-backed interest rates. The dollar is also the safe haven for many investors in many countries. There is no doubt that a stronger dollar will hurt exports, but given our trade deficit, we import more than we export, and now we do that at a cheaper price. That's good for consumers or for business (even better if they don't pass on all the savings to their customers). But U.S. companies that have large foreign income have seen profits decrease with the sudden strength in the dollar. The yin and yang out of balance again.

There is always a way of explaining the past and sounding very smart. But the winners are the ones that follow a sound systematic approach. Trends exist because there is no consensus among investors. If there were, prices would jump directly to their correct value. A divergence in two related stocks doesn't need a sophisticated analysis. The stock market has been going up for years, and if you followed the trend, you would have profited handsomely without needing to explain the fundamentals. If you keep arbing divergences and include the upward bias in your plan, the numbers will pay off for you. It's just that some traders like to have some fundamental data to help them take the trade. Trying to confirm a systematic trade with fundamentals will keep you out of many trades.

CHAPTER 6

If You're a Trend Follower, Don't Use Profit-Taking or Stops

What? Don't use stops? Don't take profits? How can I control risk? Why wouldn't I take a windfall profit? It does sound counterintuitive, but it's really simple to explain. Profit-taking and stops fight with a trend-following strategy.

Let's consider how trend following works. First, there are long-term trends that hinge on interest rate policy, which is slow moving. Very slow moving. The movement of a Central Bank makes a snail look fast. And, once it has decided on a policy, it implements it tenaciously, slowly, over and over, until it thinks it has accomplished its goal, whatever that was. All that causes trends in the interest rate markets to move slowly and last a long time. In the United States, we could say that this generation of young financial geniuses has never seen a bear market in rates. Yields have been declining, more or less, since 1980. The Eurodollar chart, Figure 6.1, shows that.

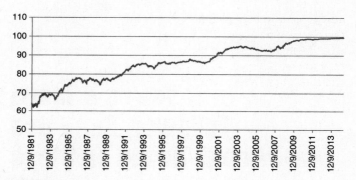

FIGURE 6.1 Eurodollar Prices from Back-Adjusted Futures

Consider our current situation. The U.S. economy is strong, the European economy is weak. The European Central Bank has just begun quantitative easing (you would think they would have done this sooner to be preemptive). This means money will flow out of Europe, which has lower interest rates, and into the United States. That money will move into U.S. government debt (for example, bonds) and the stock market, which also means that foreign investors will be buying the dollar. We should see a slow, upward pressure on both markets as this evolves. Not everyone moves his or her money the same day. The pattern, therefore, will not always be smooth.

These long-term trends are based on Central Bank action. We could put numbers around it and say that trends exist in the time frame of 40 to 250 trading days; that's two months to one year. They could be longer, but a trader doesn't care about anything slower than that. If you view it the opposite way, there are no trends of 10 or 20 days. There are often sharp, volatile moves in one direction within that time frame, but they are caused by short-term news or supply-and-demand changes. They are inconsistent in duration, most lasting a few days, others a week or two. I classify this as market noise, not trends, even though others might call them trends.

There are always exceptions. The collapse of the dot-com bubble in 2000 was not following interest rate policy, yet resulted in a huge, sustained trend. Crude oil prices, generally driven by supply and demand (and occasionally encouraged by OPEC), rose from $40 to $140 and back to near $30, another remarkable trend and best captured with a faster trend system. But these are exceptions.

While I seem to hold these long-term interest rate trends as very important, there are other major trends resulting from supply-and-demand imbalances that can be equally profitable. The most obvious have been in the energy markets, but they also occur regularly in seasonal commodities or seasonal stocks. A seasonal trend must be, by definition, much shorter than a year because they repeat each year. In fact, the idea that a stock may have a quarterly pattern based on earnings reports is coincidental with the seasonality of a commodity such as wheat, which can also be seen in quarterly moves.

If you were to apply a long-term trend to wheat, you would not see the seasonal changes but instead see the changes in the U.S. dollar. Because wheat has an international value, it rises when the dollar falls and falls when the dollar rises, so that it effectively keeps a constant world value (assuming constant world supply).

THE DYNAMICS OF A TREND STRATEGY

Regardless of long term or short term, a trend system applies the principle of "conservation of capital" because it takes a small loss when the trend fails, but holds the trade when it continues in the same direction. Over time, only about 30% of trend trades are profitable. Then, to net a profit, the profitable trades must be much larger, on average, than the losing trades.

There is one other critical dynamic. It turns out that to get long-term profits using trend following, you need to capture those trends that last a very, very long time— unpredictably and unexpectedly long. Those moves are the *fat tail*. Without the fat tail, trend following would not be profitable.

The fat tail is not predictable. The 30-year decline in interest rate yields, the move in gold to near $2,000 an ounce, the rise and fall of crude oil, the Internet bubble of the 1990s, and the financial crisis of 2008, the result of the lax standards in mortgage lending, were predictable only with hindsight.

IT'S GETTING HARDER TO FIND THE TREND

In the early 1970s, even into the 1980s and early 1990s, trading the trend was easy. When Donchian published his 10-day moving average in the 1960s (he published the 5- and 20-day trend system in 1974), it actually made money. Now, most of us know it doesn't work and seems ridiculously simple. It worked then because the markets were different. There were a larger percentage of commercials (traders who, for example, hedge manufacturing inventory), no funds as we know them today, such as PIMCO's bond fund, certainly no ETFs, and far fewer individual investors.

When prices went up, they continued to go up because most everyone had the same opinion on market direction. That's still true of new markets, which are now limited to emerging economies. But it doesn't last forever. As volume increases, it attracts more investors, and eventually attracts funds and more ambitious traders. All that adds noise to the price movement because more traders have more opinions, different time frames, and different objectives. That noise makes it difficult to identify the trend as quickly as we did in the early 1970s. We need to wait longer to be sure it's really a trend move and not a large price shock or random move. So we get into the trend later and out later, netting less from the move. Trends still exist and they're still profitable, just less so.

THE EURODOLLAR TREND

It's difficult to find a better example of a trend than short-term interest rates. We'll use the Eurodollar futures (the European interest rate for U.S. dollars deposited abroad, remembering that the yield is 100 minus the 3-month LIBOR), which is the most liquid contract in the world. From 1981 through 2014 (about 35 years), prices moved smoothly higher, as seen in Figure 6.1. Of course, if you look carefully, there were short periods of rising yields (from 2003 to 2007 prices declined), but given 35 years, it's a small correction.

If we use a simple 200-day moving average, a favorite benchmark of stock analysts, and plot the profit gained from January 2000 (a more relevant period), we find that returns are very nice, but not perfect (see Figure 6.2). Over the 15 years from then to 2014, it averaged 13.6% per year with a target risk of 12%. That's a highly desirable information ratio (*IR*, the return divided by the risk) of 1.13. Before you start saying that it's not good enough, over the same period, the SPY (sector SPDRs) had a return of only 4.1% and a risk of 20.4% for a ratio of 0.20, not quite so desirable (see Figure 6.3), and with a drawdown of more than 50%. We prefer to remember only the last five years.

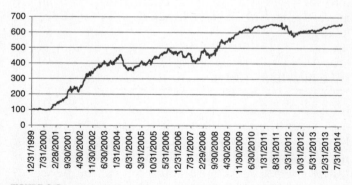

FIGURE 6.2 Eurodollar Futures NAV Using a 200-Day Moving Average

WHERE DO YOU PLACE YOUR STOP?

If you were trading the SPY with the benefit of hindsight, where would you place your stop-loss? You would certainly want to cut your 2008 losses as soon as possible, but there was another slow erosion of equity from 2000 to 2002, netting about the same loss (see Figure 6.3). And, there was another 20% loss in 2010. So, do you try to keep losses under 10% or under 20%? If you look at the returns from the 200-day moving average, you see that the biggest losses were about 20%. For a moving average system, the stop is when the trend reverses. To me, it seems like a lot less trouble to follow the trend.

Say that you've figured out the perfect place to take your loss. You decide that 12% is the sweet spot. Along with reducing the big drawdowns, you cut your loss in

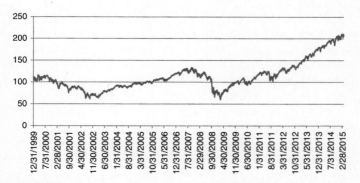

FIGURE 6.3   SPY Prices from January 1, 2000, Adjusted to 100

2010 from 20% to 12%, but the trend was still up. You need to get back into the trade or you might miss the fat tail. In fact, this time that would be right—prices kept going up. How do you get back in? You can't use the trend signal because it was long when you got out and stayed long. You need a rule that works for all the times when you were stopped out, and that could be more difficult than just staying with the original trend.

It's not that stops are wrong for all systems, but it's short sighted for a trend strategy. It looks to reduce a short-term loss by giving up a long-term profit, and it can significantly lower the percentage of good trades, which are already low for moving averages.

WHAT ABOUT PROFIT-TAKING?

As tempting as it is to take money off the table when you get a good run of profits, you face the same problem as using stops. You're out with a profit but the trend is still up. If you don't get back in, you risk missing the fat tail. It's not as though prices weren't going your way to start with. Once you're out, what are the choices for getting back in? Do you wait for a retracement to enter at a better price? That might not happen, so you also need to have a new rule that says, "Reenter if prices go higher than where I got out." Exiting at one price and reentering higher isn't going to improve your returns.

Profit-taking is a matter of managing your gains instead of managing your risk. Just as with stops, profit-taking has its place, but not in trend following. We'll discuss that in Chapter 7.

ENTERING ON A PULLBACK

There are times when you want to think like a discretionary trader. Most don't like to chase the market when they get a buy signal on rising prices. There is a good argument for waiting for a pullback, although how much of a pullback can be very subjective.

An algorithmic trader needs clear rules. One easy answer is to wait after an initial buy signal, then buy if the 2-day low is penetrated. It's just a small pullback but it will avoid chasing the market, separate you from the pack that's buying the breakout or piggy-backing on a moving average signal, and get a better price. Occasionally, you'll miss getting a better price because the price will continue higher, but not that often. You will need a rule that says, "If I don't get a better price within three days (or three hours), get in at the market."

Can you use the same approach for exits? Yes, but there's an increased risk. Personally, I like waiting for a small reversal to exit because most often it is a better fill and I'm not fighting with other systems to get through the door. But there is a caveat. Occasionally, very occasionally, you'll get stuck in a trade waiting for that pullback. You could give back a lot. In one futures portfolio that I created, there was one case over 20 years of data in one market out of 60. We got caught in the yen and took a big loss that wouldn't have happened if we had simply exited on the trend signal. Did it make a difference in the final profits of the system? No. But if you looked carefully at the trades, it was a big loss and it looked stupid. It would be difficult to explain to a client. So I use the pullback for an entry but not for an exit.

WHICH IS THE BEST
TREND-FOLLOWING METHOD?

I knew you would want to ask this, and I don't blame you. There is a difference between methods, especially a moving average, breakout, and linear regression, three popular candidates. Not surprisingly, any one of them can be best at any one time.

Let me repeat the big picture concept: If the market trends, then all trend methods make money; if the market doesn't trend, then none of the trend methods make money. So it's the market, not the method, and that leads to portfolio selection, which we'll discuss in Chapter 14.

There are differences among the three techniques, both conceptually and in the way they deal with risk:

1. A moving average takes many small losses and fewer large profits. A series of small losses can add up to a big loss. It also has an "agenda," that is, when the market goes sideways after a move up, the moving average continues to advance and eventually triggers a change of trend even though prices are actually going sideways, not reversing, and may resume their upward direction.

2. A breakout system has much better reliability. More than 50% of the trades are often profitable. To achieve that, it can have very large risks. For example, the risk of a 40-day breakout system is the difference between the 40-day high and a 40-day low. If the market has been volatile, that can be a big number. Its success is due to the timeliness of the breakout signal, which

triggers an entry on a new high, and because it allows prices to flop around while investors are trying to decide which way it should go. It's a good application of the "loose pants" philosophy.

3. The linear regression simulates a chartist drawing a line. As you move forward in time, you watch to see if the line through the price movement flattens out and then turns down. This can be done by simply looking at the slope of the line, a calculation available as a function in Excel. Its performance profile is somewhere between the moving average and the breakout.

The choice of which trend method you use is more a decision of style and risk profile, and less one of returns. My own preference is the breakout because it has lower costs (fewer trades), entry points that I can understand, and allows prices to move around without causing false signals. Despite that, I believe that most traders use moving averages. I can only guess that they think individual small losses, even when sequences of small losses can add up to a large loss, are easier to accept than a single large loss.

CHAPTER 7

Take Your Profit If You're a Short-Term Trader

As you know from the previous chapter, I don't think profit-taking works with macrotrend systems, but they are important for short-term traders, very important. At the same time, they tell you something about using stops.

Why doesn't profit-taking work for trend following? Because you cut your profits short and give up the fat tail, the extremely big profits. I talked about that in Chapter 6. But for short-term trading, there is no fat tail, only small profits and small losses. In fact, there is mostly noise. If you remember, I believe that trend following is a long-term concept and that trends don't exist in the very short term. Even if you could point to a real trend starting after a few days, the market noise is overwhelming. You would know it only after the fact. Over a few days, or a week or two, you can't separate the trend from the noise. It's only later, when the trend continues, that you can see it. Let's look at the SPY at the very bottom of the 2008 decline (Figure 7.1).

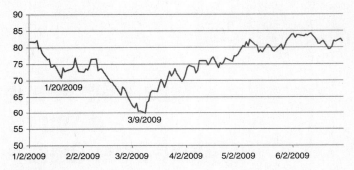

FIGURE 7.1 SPY at the Lowest Point in the Financial Crisis

Trying to be objective, prices were still falling at the beginning of 2009 and dropped another 15% in a few days, bottoming at about 70 on January 20. Do you go long on the next day, the 21st, because prices closed higher? Not likely. But then we get a bigger drop of 22%, from about 77 to 60, ending on March 9, do you go long on the next day's reversal? If you didn't go long on the 21st, then you're not doing it on the 10th. Prices go up another day. If you're a chartist, the first place to go long would be a break above 77 or 82, the two nearest resistance points. But even those are very short-term and not well-developed levels, so you would need to be aggressive to enter a long position. Had you taken this approach during the past year, you would be out of capital. Prices now start moving sideways near those two levels, making them look more important. What do you do now? Without knowing that the lows had already been seen, it's not easy to make a decision to pick the bottom after a long, steep decline.

WHAT'S BAD FOR THE TREND IS GOOD FOR THE SHORT-TERM TRADER

Have you noticed that a price chart looks more like random movement as you change the resolution from longer to shorter, that is, from weekly to daily and from daily to 5 minutes? In the short term, we see small movements in prices reflecting all of the buy-and-sell orders. As you step back, the big picture emerges, most often showing a trend. This price noise makes it difficult to identify a trend with only a small amount of data. On the other hand, short-term traders can use this random-like movement to their advantage.

In Figure 7.2, the daily crude oil prices show a steep drop from September 2008 through the end of 2008. No

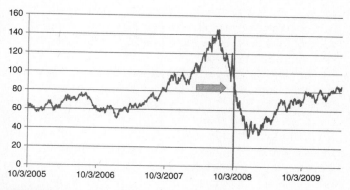

FIGURE 7.2 Crude Oil Daily Cash Prices Showing the Area of Interest

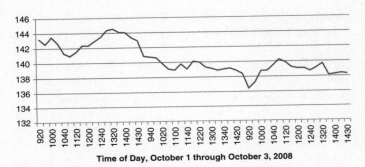

FIGURE 7.3 Crude Oil 20-Minute Futures Data

one would say that's not a trend. In Figure 7.3, we show three days from October 1 through October 3, 2008, indicated by the arrow in Figure 7.2. The longer-term chart makes it appear as though prices are in a free-fall. While there is steep downtrend, it is certainly not as uniform as you would expect. If we look closely enough, prices rarely go straight up or down.

When we're dealing with noise, we don't have high expectations of prices continuing in the same direction over the next few bars. If you're a short-term trader, it follows that if you get a larger-than-average move in your direction, then you should take at least part of your gains off the table because you expect prices to reverse. Then profit-taking is good for short-term traders, but not for long-term trend followers.

While we always want to capture the largest move possible, we don't know exactly what that is. The best measurement for targeting profits is a multiple of the average true range (ATR), which is similar to the average of the daily high-low difference, but includes that gap opening if there is one. For short-term trading, a move from the entry price of 2 to 3 ATRs is a good target. Following our philosophy that we should never hang our hat on a single number, it's best if you target three profit levels, say 1.5, 2.0, and 4.0 ATRs. That gives you an average of 2.5. The benefit of these three levels, especially with at least one likely to be reached, is that you reduce your exposure and risk for every profit level captured. If you can capture two levels, then it will be very difficult to turn a profit into a loss. Think of it as additional diversification.

Be sure you use a Limit Order to capture the profit target as it happens. If you're right, the price may not stay there for long.

IF YOU CAN'T USE STOPS FOR TREND FOLLOWING, CAN YOU USE THEM FOR SHORT-TERM TRADING?

So what about stops? First, let's assume you are going to use a stop-loss order. Do you enter it as a Stop Order? That means it will be executed "at the market" if the price is hit. If you reverse the logic we just used for profit-taking, which was that you want to take profits as soon as the price is reached because the price won't keep going in that direction, then you don't want to exit on a stop because prices will also reverse. Instead, know where your stop is, but wait until after it has penetrated to execute. If it's an intraday stop, then exit on the close. It sounds as though you're exposing yourself to more risk, but you're taking advantage of more short-term market noise. It will work most of the time.

That's not to say that I like stops. I think they interfere with the underlying strategy, and are often based on how much you are willing to lose and less about what latitude the system needs to succeed. Because there are so many short-term trades, you can always try to make it up on the next trade.

If you have a mean-reversion or arbitrage strategy, its profile will be a lot of small profits and a few large losses. When you add a stop-loss, you reduce the high percentage of small profitable trades and upset the balance. You can turn a profitable system into a losing one.

In general, if you think the risk of a system is larger than your comfort level, then trade a smaller position. Don't add artificial risk controls.

THERE ARE ALWAYS EXCEPTIONS

One example where a stop is needed is in pairs trading, a popular type of stock arbitrage. You find two related stocks, say Pfizer and Merck, and wait for prices to diverge more than usual. You can do that simply by looking at the standard deviation of the ratio of the two prices. When they are far enough apart, you buy the cheap one (Pfizer) and sell the expensive one (Merck). You hold until the ratio goes back to normal, which would be the average ratio.

But what happens if Pfizer is sued by the government for a drug that has harmed millions of people? The price of Pfizer plummets. You are long Pfizer because it has turned lower pending the outcome of a new study. You have no protection because it looks like an even a better buy to the system. In this case, it is necessary to place a stop 10% to 20% below the entry price of the long leg of the trade (Pfizer). It must be far enough away to be sure something is wrong, but close enough to avoid a large loss.

If there is a natural stop in the system, then a protective stop, as in our Pfizer example, shouldn't be used. For trend following, the stop is when the trend changes direction. For a classic divergence pattern, the exit is when the divergence disappears. Again, if the risk is too high, trade a smaller position, but stay with the system.

CHAPTER 8

Searching for the Perfect System

What is a perfect system and how do you find it? I don't think you'll find two people who agree on that, unless there is a strategy that has only profits and no losses. It's not likely you're going to find that one.

Many years ago, when we were having a good run of performance, lots of profits and a few reasonable, not scary, losses, one of our clients called and explained very seriously that he would be willing to give up some of the profits if we could eliminate all of the losses. A nice thought, but as we say, "Not clear on the concept."

Every trader has a different tolerance for risk and each needs to find a method that minimizes his or her anxiety. I think the anxiety is more important than the potential gain. You'll never realize the gain if you can't stay with the program.

Let's be realistic. Finding the best system involves back-testing. If you're an algorithmic trader, you can program and test the exact rules. If you're a systematic trader (discretionary but with clear rules in mind), then you look for past scenarios to confirm your method. It's not scientific, but it may be the best you can do.

The purpose is clearly to confirm your idea, and the best way is to see how it did in the past. If it flopped badly, why would you trade it? Working in the past doesn't mean that it will work in the future, but at least it needs to validate your idea of past price action.

Let's summarize what we've discussed in the previous sections:

- Start with a sound premise. You need an idea, a concept, based on something fundamentally sensible, such as interest rate policy or seasonality.
- Choose a range of parameters that also fit the concept, including the time period (long-term or short-term), and frequency of data (15 minute, daily, weekly).
- Set your expectations in advance. Do you expect to have many small profits and a few large losses, a few large profits and a lot of small losses, or something in between? Should it return 6% annually, as with merger arb, or 20% for leveraged futures?
- What markets should it work on? If it's a long-term trend system based on interest rate policy, then it should work on the longer maturity rates. If it's a short-term mean reversion approach, then you'll want the noisier equity index markets, or possibly fast-moving, low-priced stocks. Even if you plan to trade only a single stock, like Apple, is there another company that has the same characteristics, or had those characteristics at one time, such as Google, Microsoft, or even Amazon, when they started gaining traction? Testing only one market is risky because it may not include enough real-life events.

LOOKING AT THE RESULTS

We program our idea into a spreadsheet or testing platform, any one of them will do, and we run a series of tests.
We use realistic costs. What do we find out?

1. Every combination of parameters and rules makes
   money. I would suggest that you look for an error in
   your test, such as using today's data to predict yesterday. Nothing could ever be that good.
2. All of them lose money. Perhaps your costs are too
   high or you have an error in your rules. But it is possible that prices move in the opposite way from what
   you expected. That could be good news.
3. A sequence of tests makes money, but larger groups are
   net losses (a very likely outcome).
4. A large majority of tests are profitable, but the results
   vary quite a bit. Some are excellent and some barely
   break even. The best results seem to cluster and taper
   off at the edges, somewhat like a relief map. (This is a
   very good result.)

The last case is the best you should expect. Only long-
term trend following has shown to be profitable in a wide
range of medium-to-slow trends, which is why it's used
by so many professional managers. But if you understand
your strategy, and define your expectations correctly, many
of the parameters tested can be profitable.

Let's first look at Case 3. You've tested 1,000 combinations and tests number 600 to 800 look good enough to
trade. The others are near break even or losses. You ask

yourself, "Is this simply the sweet spot?" It's possible but not likely. Remember, you defined the range of parameters and rules in advance, with the idea that you were validating them using testing. If 20% of the tests are profitable, that's not good enough. Or if the profitable cases are scattered around in some random way, it's not good. Consider the extreme: if 999 of the 1,000 tests lost money, but 1 test had only profitable trades. It was perfect, but would you consider that a success? I hope not.

Let's look at Case 4. A lot of positive results are great, and clustering is also good. Expecting high returns everywhere is asking too much. If we were to look at the results on a yearly basis, we would expect the best performance will jump around, depending on the way prices move and the trend develops. A very strong trend favors slow trading while more price reversals can shift profits to the shorter calculation periods.

HOW MUCH DATA AND HOW MANY TRADES ARE ENOUGH?

I've mentioned before that more data is better. It needs to include bull markets, bear markets, and sideways markets. The more data, the more patterns and price shocks, so future results will be more predictable, although far from perfect.

The number of trades in your test is equally as important. Again, the more trades, the better. For short-term traders, that's easy. If your trade lasts no more than three days and you have 40 trades each year, then you're in the market 120 days, about half the time. If you test 10 years of data, you have 400 trades. According to the formula for sample error (1 divided by the square root of the number of trades), that's a 5% error. It would be nice if it were smaller, but 5% is considered the minimum acceptable confidence level.

Trend-following tests are a problem. If you use a 200-day moving average over 10 years of data, you are lucky to get 5 trades per year. That's 50 trades with a sample error of 14%. Not good enough. For futures, there is data going back to 1990 for most markets, but a typical database of stocks will only have 15 years of past data. With 5 trades each year, using all the data will improve the error to 11%.

Accepting results based on lower confidence becomes a leap of faith. For a long-term trend follower who believes that trends are based on both interest rate policy and supply-and-demand factors, that leap may not be big. For a pattern trader looking for something very specific that happens only a few times each year, fewer trades will be a problem. For those programs, using out-of-sample data or paper trading will be the only way to validate the results and avoid real trading losses.

SO, WHICH PARAMETER VALUE DO I PICK?

We can't expect one set of parameters, even the one that shows the best long-term returns, to have been the best each year. It's unrealistic. Choosing a single parameter set to trade is the same as choosing a single stock to trade. You have the greatest chance of the biggest return but also the greatest chance of the biggest loss. By trading two stocks that are not similar, you get an average return and a much lower risk.

It's the same with parameter selection. Trade a system with a single trend calculation period and you can be a big winner or a big loser. Trade the same system with two time periods (for example, a 40- and 80-day trend) and you smooth out the results. Then choosing three or four different parameter combinations gives you a more stable return. We'll go into this in more detail in the next chapter.

CHAPTER 9

Equal Opportunity Trading

All things being equal, the individual investor can do a better job getting diversification and controlling risk than the big players because it's easier to manage a small amount of capital. Risk needs to be controlled. Losing sight of it can be fatal to your investments.

Hedge funds with enormous amounts of assets under management, such as ED&F Man, will find it very difficult to diversify. They are limited by market liquidity and will seek out the cash markets to spread their risk more effectively. For these firms, diversification is limited.

For the rest of us, to control risk properly, you must start by taking positions with equal risk. That's equal risk, not equal expectations of reward, or some risk-reward combination. It's only the risk that matters. The purpose is to give each trade an equal chance to participate in the returns. If you have twice as much exposure on one stock that you believe has a better chance of a profit, then it had better return twice the average, or you've only increased your risk.

With all due respect, picking stocks in order of expected return is a pretty tricky process, even if you use a well-known ranking service, such as Starmine. Among the top 5 or 10 highest-ranked stocks, can you tell which will have the highest return in the next week or the next trade? It's very unlikely. So staying with equal risk is going to be safer and easier.

CALCULATING POSITION SIZE

It's not complicated to calculate the position size because there is very little choice. If you're a stock trader, then simply divide your investment equally into the number of stocks you trade, so a $100,000 investment will allow $10,000 for each of 10 stocks. Not rocket science. When you take a position, divide the $10,000 by the stock price. It's not perfect, but generally a higher-price stock has a larger price range, so this will be a sloppy way of adjusting each position to an equal dollar risk.

AVOID LOW-PRICED STOCKS

To be perfectly accurate, higher-priced stocks have much larger trading ranges than lower-priced stocks, but not in percentage terms. Just the opposite is true. There is a tendency for the percentage daily volatility to increase slightly as prices move lower. But when a stock price declines from normal to very low because of some company-related problem, it becomes exceptionally volatile. You cannot size a position in a stock that has just dropped from $30 to $5 and expect it to mix in your portfolio. It's just too volatile. The easiest solution is to remove any stock priced below $5 from your portfolio. We'll discuss this more in Chapter 13.

TRUE VOLATILITY-ADJUSTING DOESN'T WORK FOR A PORTFOLIO OF STOCKS

It would be better if we could volatility-adjust the position sizes in stocks as we can in futures. Futures allow varying leverage and are normally traded with a large part of the investment set aside as a reserve to absorb losses. In stocks, if your selection includes one with low volatility, you would need to trade more than the $10,000 allocation (our preceding example) to bring that volatility up to match the other stocks, and that's not possible without investing more money. You could reduce the position size in the other stocks until you have the same volatility as the lowest stock, but then you're not using all the money and your returns will be smaller. So it's a dilemma. My experience is that simply dividing an equal investment by the stock price is as close as you'll get to an answer.

RISK IN FUTURES

Futures allow you to use real volatility parity. To calculate the volatility, which is the same as the risk, find the 20-day ATR (Average True Range) of the daily prices. Choose an arbitrary investment amount for each market, say $25,000, and divide that investment by the dollar value of the volatility. You'll get larger sizes for markets with lower volatility (usually the interest rates), and smaller sizes for more volatile markets (equity index and crude oil). Then you need to scale all position sizes up or down, in the same proportion, to match your actual investment.

For example, we do our position sizing in futures based on a $25,000 investment, and get 5 contracts for the current crude oil trade. We have a total of 10 markets that we plan to trade, which would mean that we needed a total investment of $250,000. But we only use $100,000, or 40% of that nominal value (the balance is held in reserve). We simply take 40% of the position size, or 2 contracts instead of 5.

TARGET RISK

The *target risk* is the amount of risk you are willing to take. It's a more difficult concept for some investors because it's not an absolute number and it is most often used for futures trading. You might invest $100,000 and be willing to lose $20,000, or 20%, but deciding your position size to find the right balance of maximizing returns and not losing more than 20% is a problem in probability. But not a complicated one.

First, we need to find out how much risk you have based on the position sizes for your investment, which we calculated earlier. Using a spreadsheet (see Table 9.1), the dates will be in the first column, then each other column will be the daily returns of each market you are trading using the number of contracts that we have assigned. For simplicity, let's just use the SPY prices.

Put the date and closing price in columns A and B. Calculate the daily return, B3/B2–1 in C3. Copy down column C. To get the rolling, 20-day annualized volatility, put STDEV(C3:C22)*SQRT(252) in cell D22 and copy down. If you plot column D, you'll get the annualized volatility. If you do this for your portfolio returns, you will have the rolling volatility of your own trading. In Table 9.1, the volatility starts at 8.7% and increases to 13.7% in only 18 days.

Using your own trading, you have daily profits and losses, in dollars, rather than percentage returns. In column F of the spreadsheet we show the number of SPY shares that you might hold on any one day. The profit (or loss) for that day is the number of shares × (today's price – the previous price), which we put into column G. You calculate the annualized risk using all the daily profits and losses, not just 20 days.

Say that your annualized risk is $2,040, shown at the bottom of column G. If you want a target risk of 12%, divide the 2,040 by 0.12 to get $17,003. That's the investment needed to have a risk of 12%. If you have $100,000, then the risk of the current portfolio is 2,040/100,000, or 2%. You'll need to increase the size of your positions by a multiple of 5.88 to reach your target volatility. For stocks, you'll need to be sure you have excess liquidity.

CALCULATE THE RATE OF RETURN FOR THE PORTFOLIO

You can go back now and use column E in Table 9.1 to create the Net Asset Value from the percentage returns. For your own portfolio, divide each daily profit (column G) by

TABLE 9.1 Calculating the AROR, Volatility, and Information Ratio

A Date	B SPY	C Return	D Vol	E NAV	F Shares	G $Profit
3/6/2015	206.58	-0.01403	0.087860	186.1752	48	-140.32
3/9/2015	207.43	0.00411	0.088037	186.9412	48	41.15
3/10/2015	204.07	-0.01620	0.105292	183.9131	49	-161.98
3/11/2015	203.59	-0.00235	0.097876	183.4805	49	-23.52
3/12/2015	206.18	0.01272	0.108623	185.8147	49	127.22
3/13/2015	204.92	-0.00611	0.104554	184.6792	49	-61.11
3/16/2015	207.65	0.01332	0.114800	187.1395	48	133.22
3/17/2015	207.04	-0.00294	0.114958	186.5898	48	-29.38
3/18/2015	209.52	0.01198	0.123202	188.8248	48	119.78

(Continued)

70

TABLE 9.1 Continued

A Date	B SPY	C Return	D Vol	E NAV	F Shares	G $Profit
3/19/2015	208.57	-0.00453	0.124280	187.9686	48	-45.34
3/20/2015	210.41	0.00882	0.126509	189.6269	48	88.22
3/23/2015	210.00	-0.00195	0.126709	189.2574	48	-19.49
3/24/2015	208.82	-0.00562	0.127714	188.1939	48	-56.19
3/25/2015	205.76	-0.01465	0.137315	185.4362	49	-146.54
3/26/2015	205.27	-0.00238	0.137385	184.9946	49	-23.81
3/27/2015	205.74	0.00229	0.137660	185.4182	49	22.90

			AROR »	0.041		2,040
			Ratio »	0.203		17,003

Vol »	0.204

the investment size to get the daily returns. We'll continue to use the returns of SPY for convenience.

Start with 100 in E2. Then E3 = E2*(1 + C2), where E2 is the previous NAV and C2 is the current return. Copy down Column E. You can plot the NAV.

If there are 500 rows, the annualized rate of return (AROR) is

$$AROR = (E500/E2)^{\wedge}(252/years) - 1$$

where E500 is the last NAV, E2 is the first NAV (usually 100), and *years* is the number of years expressed as a decimal number (for example, 2 ½ years is 2.5). Using SPY data from January 1, 2000, the AROR is 4.1%. Try it yourself to be sure that you have it right. You should have a lot of use for it.

ASSIGNING RISK TO YOUR PORTFOLIO

The typical professionally managed futures account targets a volatility of 12%. That means that there is a 16% chance of losing more than 12% in one year, which should have occurred over the life of the data that you've just used to calculate the numbers.

Without getting complicated, the 16% comes from the distribution of one standard deviation, which represents about 68% of the data in the middle of a bell curve. That leaves 16% on either side, but we're only interested in the left, which shows losses. It also means that there is a 16% chance of a profit greater than 12%. While it's not true that the data is as uniform as a bell curve, financial analysts use it anyway as a way of representing risk. Simple is better, or at least convenient.

If you're more aggressive, you will want a 14% or 16% target, but not higher. If you're conservative, it will be 10% or 8%, rarely lower. If the current volatility is 18% and you want 10%, then you simply reduce your position size by a factor of 10/18 or raise your investment by a factor of 18/10.

For futures, a 12% target volatility translates into leverage of about 12:1.

An important extra is that portfolio volatility needs to be adjusted up and down from time to time. When all the markets in the portfolio are quiet, you need to leverage up the positions to your target volatility. It turns out that good performance often occurs at low volatility, but your returns are also low. By increasing all the positions in your futures portfolio equally, you can greatly increase your long-term performance without going above your target risk. If you don't increase your leverage, you'll wonder why you're underperforming.

When varying the leverage, don't make small changes because they will increase the cost of trading unnecessarily. Wait until the volatility changes by 10%, or even 20%, before adding or removing contracts. Even simply adjusting once a month is better than not at all.

MULTIPLE STRATEGIES ARE MORE IMPORTANT

In the scheme of risk control, diversifying into more than one strategy is more important than diversification across markets. Look back at 2008, an important lesson. When the financial crisis of 2008–2009 was in full bloom, everyone was running for the door. If you were long, you sold, and if you were short, you bought. If you had physical commodities, such as gold or silver, you sold to cover losses. So everything reversed at the same time. In statistics, we say that all correlations went to 1, that is, they all moved in the same direction at the same time. In truth, they all reversed at the same time.

A safer way to gain diversification is with different strategies. If you have a long-term trend system and a short-term mean reversion system, they will be holding different positions most of the time—but not always. Even with random coin flips, there is a 25% chance that two coins will get the same heads or tails. If you are trading long only, you also lower the odds of diversification. But diverse systems are still a far better alternative than trading only stocks or futures using one method.

Think of strategy diversification in the same way as market diversification. If you trade only one stock, you can get the biggest return or the biggest risk. If you trade two stocks, you get the average return and a lower risk. The lower risk depends on how different the signals are for the two stocks. Trading Hewlett-Packard and Dell would not give much diversification, but General Electric and Facebook would be quite different.

The magic number for diversification is four. After you have four different strategies, you reach diminishing returns, more or less. That is, adding a fifth strategy offers only a 20% improvement, even if that strategy is really unique. The biggest improvement is in the first three or four.

NOT SO EASY FOR THE INSTITUTIONS

Most everyone can allocate equal risk to every trade, but allocating an equal investment to every market is a problem for the large, institutional traders. Not all stocks can handle the same size investment if you're trying to keep your position size under, say, 3% of the daily volume. Even with a VWAP (Volume Weighted Average Price), or entering over a number of days, you still bump up against liquidity constraints.

It's the exits that really tell you when your position size is too big, because you're going to be in more of a hurry to close out a bad position. You can use clever timing rules for entering but, as the old phrase goes, "I didn't pay to get in, but where do I pay to get out?" Institutional investors will seek as many markets as possible to offset the lack of liquidity. Individual investors don't have that problem.

TOO MUCH OF A GOOD THING CAN BE BAD

In theory, the more diversification you have, the lower your risk. It is also true that your returns are lower because they are the average of everything you are trading. The standing explanation for diversifying into many stocks or futures markets is that we don't know which one is going to produce the next big profit, so we need to trade as many markets as possible. That's both true and false.

If you're a trend follower, sometimes the markets don't trend. If you're a mean reversion trader, sometimes they do trend. Both are bad. When it goes on that way for a long time, your equity declines steadily. Yet among the hundreds of stocks and dozens of futures markets, there are usually some that are doing well for your trading method. Is it possible to select those that will be profitable and ignore the others? It sounds like a fool's errand.

Sometimes it's easier to prove a point by showing a very small case. For example, if you have a futures portfolio with six sectors, interest rates, equity index, FX, energy, metals, and agricultural products, is it likely that one of those groups is performing better than the others? Of course. Is one doing much worse? Yes. How about silver? My own opinion is that silver is the poor man's gold. It's lagged far behind when gold made its move to $2,000, but has come back down along with gold. Figure 9.1 shows that silver tracks gold, but Figure 9.2, the ratio of gold to silver, shows how unstable that relationship is. At one time, silver stayed very close to a 33:1 ratio with gold. At 60:1 it's now fallen to half that value and varies erratically. I know of no system that can make money in silver over the long term.

If I can just eliminate silver from my diversified portfolio, then the average returns will go up. Yes, I will lose some amount of diversification, but it contributes only losses. I don't know of any examples, other than academic ones, where you can add a losing asset and have your portfolio improve.

We've then decided that we can remove those markets that perform terribly, or "robustly bad." That improves results. If we can show that there is persistence in good

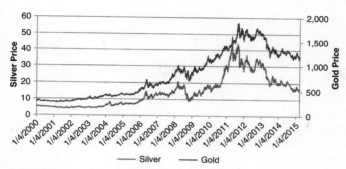

FIGURE 9.1   Cash Silver and Gold Prices

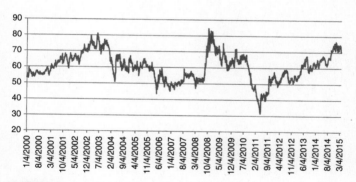

FIGURE 9.2   Gold-Silver Ratio

performance, that is, a stock or bond that is doing well is likely to continue to do well, we have a tool that can then be used for selection.

There is also the issue of over-diversification. At some point, adding more markets will include those with marginal returns. That can lower your expected returns to an undesirable level. If you don't need more systems or markets, don't add them.

Because this chapter was about equal risk, we'll defer the portfolio selection to Chapter 14, where we discuss it in more detail.

CHAPTER 10

Testing—The Fork in the Road

We've talked about testing already, but in generalities. It's time for some clarity.

Testing is a necessary evil, so it's best if you know the good and the bad of it. It is the development stage that can make you a success or turn a good idea into a failure. Only systematic traders can test properly because everything has been set down in clear rules. Putting your idea into a spreadsheet or programming it into a test platform, such as TradeStation, is a good way to audit yourself. You never realize what you've left out until it's written down completely and you try following your own rules. Programming those rules is a sure way of doing that. Programming it in two different platforms, and comparing the results, is even a better way of avoiding errors.

There is as much discipline needed to control your testing as there is in trading. Computers are powerful and can just as easily give you the wrong answers as the right ones. They simply respond to what you ask. It's very tempting to let the computer do more work and you do less, but that's a mistake. I'll try to show you the right way.

Start with a few basic principles:

- *More data is better.* There is no such thing as bad data. The more data, the more market situations, bull and bear trends, price shocks, and sideways periods. They all need to be part of your test.
- *Leave some data out for validation at the end.* It's your reality check. Some analysts leave out the most recent data. I prefer to alternate every two years, so that when markets change over time, I get a fair sample of that change. So I use two years, skip two years, and so on. It's a bit trickier to set up, but worth the effort.
- *Know in advance how you're going to evaluate the results.* I use the information ratio as my main criterion, but most often analysts add other criteria, such as maximum drawdown and time to recovery. I still believe that the more conditions you put on your analysis, the less chance it will work.
- *Use percentage-spaced test values.* For the most part, equally spaced values will favor either the fast or slow trading. For example, testing a trend from 10 to 200 in steps of 10 will favor the slow periods. Note that the difference between a 10- and 15-day moving average is 50%, but the difference between a 190- and 200-day average is about 2.5%. The results of a 10- and 15-day trend will be very different, but the results of a 195- and 200-day trend may be identical. When you look at the big picture of the results, it will appear that the slow trends are more stable. Instead, increase the test values by a percentage to get a better distribution.

- *Don't shotgun.* That is, don't try every parameter value possible or every possible indicator in the hope that one will be great. Statistically, if you try enough combinations, some of them are likely to work just by chance. They won't have any predictive value. Remember, the more rules, the less likely the system will work. Define the range of values, the markets, and the methods in advance. If those fail, then your concept doesn't work.

- *Reject new rules if your improvement is only marginal.* And the improvement must be based on the average of all tests, not just a single, better result. We are seeking robustness, not overfitting.

- The hardest part: *No feedback* is allowed once you've tested the data that was put aside for validation. If it didn't work, it didn't work. You're done, at least in theory. More about this later.

Let's talk more about the points that are not obvious.

LET THE COMPUTER SOLVE IT FOR YOU

In the age of increasingly powerful computers, you would think that throwing everything into a pot and letting a program sort out the rules would be the best solution. In fact, I've seen that happen with genetic algorithms and neural networks, two exceptionally powerful tools. In each case, you can enter your data, along with all possible trading rules, and these search methods will find the absolute best combinations to make the most money—naturally, in the past.

The genetic algorithm mixes and matches rules in a clever way, remembering rules that performed better and trying other rules at random, looking for a better result. It actually reflects the way nature works, introducing a mutation that turns out to be good, then propagating it so it eventually becomes the norm.

The neural network simulates the way paths work in the brain, allowing some rules to pass through to the next level if they are profitable, or blocking them if they are not. It can also put greater weight on different rules, just as our own reasoning process might work, deciding that the employment report is more important than the revised GDP.

I've been impressed by both these methods, even if they don't work for our purposes. I'm reminded of a report put out by a weather expert many years ago, who discovered that, over 18 years, a good wheat crop in Argentina was followed every year by a good harvest in England and northern Europe. Looking further, he found that the warm Gulf Stream that flowed from the eastern shore of South America to the western coast of Europe was the reason. It sounded logical but, as it turned out, not true.

Given enough data, you can always find a relationship that seems consistent. Just like the daily business news on television, you can explain what happened yesterday in such a way that you always seem very smart. That's not the same as predicting.

You can even use in-sample and out-of-sample results and be fooled. Given enough combinations, you will find one that worked well on the test data and then on the out-of-sample data. It's only a matter of doing enough tests.

The solution is to start with a sound premise, not one that explains your test results in retrospect.

HOW DO YOU EVALUATE THE RESULTS?

Using a broad brush, the way I measure robustness is the percentage of profitable results in my backtest. It doesn't matter how profitable, just that the combination of parameters gave a positive payout, net of costs. That means you want to define the range of parameters carefully so that you don't include a lot of combinations that you're pretty sure won't work. For example, with trend following, I would start with a 40-day calculation period and go up. That's because I don't believe there are consistent trends in the short term. Remember, I believe that many trends are driven by interest rate policy, and that's a long-term event.

For short-term trading, I like 15-minute data and a holding period of 3 to 5 days. If the test results show that I'm holding a trade for a month, something is wrong.

If 70% of all tests combinations are profitable, I'm successful. That's a difficult number to achieve. However, in Chapter 4, I showed that trend following can reach that goal (see the sections on *robustness*). So can pairs trading, which is stock arbitrage. If you are testing 20 trend speeds, 10 stops levels, and 10 profit-taking levels, you have 2,000 tests (they add up quickly). My rule is that 1,400 of them must be profitable, but I can be convinced that 50% is okay if there is a smooth pattern and a clustering of good returns. It just means that you overestimated the range of parameters that would work. We need to be both realistic and flexible.

WHAT'S FEEDBACK?

Feedback is cheating. You test your idea and it doesn't work as well as you expected, so you look through the trades and find that you weren't protected when the Fed finally decided they would raise rates. Bonds fell and you were long, taking a 7% loss that day. Not good. You could have used a stop, or you could have exited because volatility was very low the previous few days in anticipation of an announcement. You decide to add a 1-day stop of 3.0% because the largest 1-day loss, exclusive of the 7%, was 2.5%. That improves your performance.

The problem is that the next time the loss will be 3.1%, immediately followed by a reversal that changes the trend position from a loss to a profit, but you will have captured the loss. You can't keep studying the tested performance and fixing little pieces. It's overfitting and it doesn't work. It's just what the government does.

Consider the financial crisis again. The government plan to avoid the next crisis was:

- Break up banks that were "too big to fail" (this never happened).
- Pass a bill that requires banks to be more capitalized (Dodd-Frank).
- Micromanage other risk controls relating to the crisis (the Volcker Rule).

The government is always coming to the party late. It's certainly likely that, if they don't react to the problem, then the same thing will happen again. On the other hand, they have a false sense of security, thinking that they have removed the chance of another big crisis. Of course, that's not true. The next crisis will start with something completely different and will be just as bad.

In the same way, you can't remove the risk of a single event and expect that to prevent future risks. That's not the solution. The solution is to understand the real risks and manage them. If the risk is too big, trade a smaller position.

In 1998, Long-Term Capital Management imploded. One must say that they did it with style, supported all the way down by two Nobel Prize winners in economics and financed by a consortium of banks. According to the way I understood Lowenstein's book, *When Genius Failed*, these pillars of knowledge decided that certain events were not going to happen again; therefore, they removed the data that reflected them (the data that would have caused large losses), giving the trading program the appearance of exceptionally consistent, smooth returns. Because losses were small and the principals well-connected, they were able to get the banks to lend them money to trade and allow them to leverage the portfolio 50:1. Their arbitrage program worked for nearly five years until an "unexpected" event occurred in the Russian ruble that wiped them out. Naturally, it wasn't their fault. They argued that they had no way of predicting it because that particular event had never happened before. Hmmm.

If you fiddle with the data, or create rules to avoid historic losses, then future losses will be entirely your fault— and it's your money.

HIDDEN DANGER

I'm going to visit and revisit price shocks from time to time because they are very important and they can get lost in the mass of testing. In my opinion, most traders lose their money because they have misunderstood and underestimated the importance of price shocks.

We all know that price shocks are, by definition, unpredictable. The size of the move can be attributed to whether the surprise is bullish or bearish and the net holdings of the participants. For example, most investors are long equities. If we use the S&P as an example, when a surprisingly bad economic report comes out (assuming that's bad news), the S&P will drop sharply. If it's surprisingly good news, it will rise but not by as much. The asymmetry is because most investors are long and won't add to their positions on good news, but may liquidate on bad news. Even hedge funds are biased to the long side because the U.S. equity markets are biased long, so they may get stopped out on a sharp move lower but do nothing on a higher price jump.

FORGOTTEN HISTORY

Now we look at how price shocks are handled when developing a trading strategy, particularly when testing. As surprising as a price shock was at the time it happened, it is completely forgotten when it becomes part of the data history. This is a problem with all strategies, but more so with trend systems.

Let's say we do a simple historical test of a moving average system, with calculation periods from 20 to 200 days and normal buy-and-sell rules. Along with the typical daily price moves, the results will reflect profits and losses from price shocks, big and small. When you choose a calculation period for your trading, it is based on the best profit or the best return-to-risk ratio. It is very likely that selection will reflect the most profits, or the least losses, from price shocks. Because price shocks are unpredictable, we cannot expect more than 50% of them to be favorable, and if you're a trend follower, perhaps a much lower percentage.

Does that really make a difference? Yes. If you can't expect to profit from more than 50% of the price shocks, and that's optimistic, then if you profited from 65% of them, the profits from the 15% difference should be reversed to reflect losses. That will reduce the total return, but more important, it will increase the expected risk. It is understating the risk that gets most traders into trouble and may ultimately end their career.

Do your own calculations. Isolate the price shocks by comparing the daily range against the average daily range. If today's range is at least 2.5 times the average range, then it's a price shock. Count how many of them were favorable and find the total gains from those shocks. Then figure out the net returns if you reversed those gains in order to have only 50% favorable shocks, or 40%. It isn't as important if the returns are lower; it is most important that the risk is higher.

USE TRUE COSTS

Being conservative is a good general practice, but not when it comes to the cost of trading. Costs include commissions, slippage, and funding (if you're borrowing money). It is very important to use your best estimate of actual costs so that you get a realistic result.

If you use costs that are too high, most short-term systems will fail. If you use costs that are too low, you may be trading a system that can't net a profit. Realistic costs are best found by actual trading. If that's not possible, try to find someone who trades about the same size positions and use his or her estimates. There are people willing to share information if you ask. If you use a live account executive at a brokerage firm, he or she can often get those numbers for you.

Normally, countertrend trading has less slippage than trend trading, but there is always an exception. If you trade a large position, then you always drive the market away from you. These days, most order entry systems have "smart execution." They don't drop the whole order on the market at the same time; they try to hit the bid or offer until they fill the whole order. That's generally very good and far better than what we used to get when it was filled by a floor broker whose only legal obligation was an execution within the next 15 minutes.

If you're buying new shares and selling out of some old positions, I have found that, as a general rule, buy first if the market is opening lower, then sell a little later, or sell first if the market is opening higher. That's the way most floor traders do it. They are always on the opposite side of the retail trader and usually profitable. There are times when the market opens higher and takes off, but it's far less common than prices reversing after the open.

For those trading futures, the open is no longer in the morning, and the burst of volume we always associated with the open is no longer expected. Nearly all futures open a half hour after the close on electronic exchanges. That evening open is convenient if you're rebalancing a position, and it is most often at about the same price as the previous close (except, perhaps, on Sunday evening). Expecting a reversal after the electronic open is less likely because it's often quiet on low volume.

Instead, try trading at 8:20 A.M. New York time. That's before the economic reports are released, which is usually at 8:30 A.M. or later. It's the time that the interest rate futures used to open. My experience is that the reaction from economic reports is usually favorable for system trading. Very few reports actually cause a price shock, although a few will result in high volatility for an hour or so. It's also when volume picks up.

USE DIRTY DATA

We learn best by trial and error. I used to think that I would be perfect at programming once I made every error because I wouldn't repeat them. There is some truth in that, but not enough. There are too many possible errors, and sometimes they are disguised, so you don't recognize one that you've seen before. Still, we get better, even if it's a struggle.

I spent a good deal of time developing a short-term trading system for crude oil. That was in the early 2000s when electronic trading was just being developed. I bought 5-minute data from CQG, an excellent source. They clean all the data so the bad ticks are gone. I used that data to develop the strategy and the results were fabulous. I couldn't wait to start trading.

The system that I had developed had an 80% success rate. That's typical of an arbitrage or a short-term mean reversion program. But my first trade was a loss. No problem. Then my second trade was a loss, and my third, and my fourth. After a week, my equity was heading straight south. Clearly something was wrong, so I stopped trading in order to regroup.

The problem, as it turned out, was that there were a lot of errors in real crude oil prices, many of them small, but some big, because prices were entered manually in the pit. When activity was high, right after an API report on Wednesday (it's now released on Tuesday), the clerks entering the data lagged behind and made some errors. For example, if prices were trading at 39.98, 39.97, 39.98, 40.00, 39.99, sometimes the 40.00 was entered as 39.00. The clerk entering prices still had his fingers on the old keys. That's easy to understand if you're not an algorithmic system that sees only prices, not people. So a bad trade was triggered even though the fill would have been 40.00 and not 39.00. A small loss and an added commission, but it happened often, generating a lot of incorrect trades.

The solution is to always test what you're trading. Clean data seems best but it's not. And a system needs to be able to make money on unexpected market noise, not just on smooth, scrubbed data. That's why building your system on one set of data but testing on others is so important. If you're developing something on the U.S. 10-year note, don't let someone tell you, "Oh, don't worry about it not working on the bund because it's a different type of market." Wrong. And don't let them say, "That data is too old. It's not good anymore." Also wrong. The more you have, the better.

BACK-ADJUSTED AND SPLIT-ADJUSTED DATA

Data can present other hidden problems. The most important have to do with back-adjusting the data for stocks splits and combining contracts for longer, continuous futures prices.

It's not that there's anything wrong with the data, it's just that the older prices aren't the prices that occurred at that time. This presents a few technical problems:

1. You can't compare the high of today with a past high. While today's price is correct, past prices have changed.
2. You can't use percentages when creating trading rules. Because past data has changed, the percentages are different.
3. Futures data, and some stock data, may have negative prices for older data. In futures, where there is a positive carry for interest rates (the closing price of each new month is normally lower than the old contract), the old data are shifted down. After enough years, the price can be negative. Given the adjustments to Apple (AAPL), that price data goes negative for all data before 2005. For calculating volatility, the average true range (ATR) works, but not percentages used in the annualized volatility calculations.

THE DIFFERENT PERFORMANCE MEASURES

To decide on robustness, we've simply looked at what percentage of the tests was profitable, by any amount. But what about comparing one method to another? If you're comparing optimizations, then the one that is more robust, that is, has the largest percentage of profitable tests, would be the best choice.

There are countless other measures of performance beside profits, and they could add another dimension to comparing one strategy to another. The one I use is the information ratio (IR), which I mentioned earlier. It's a simple calculation on a spreadsheet and allows you to compare the amount of return that you get for each unit of risk. In an earlier example (in Chapter 9), I showed a spreadsheet in which we calculated the annualized risk (annualized volatility) and the AROR. The information ratio is the AROR divided by the annualized risk. If you've heard of the Sharpe ratio, it is a simple variation,

Sharpe ratio = (AROR – risk free return)/Annualized risk

Realistically, no one uses the risk-free return, and when you're comparing one system against another, it's unnecessary. You're going to use this calculation a lot, so try it on a spreadsheet. By the way, if the AROR is negative, most ratios don't give you a meaningful value.

INTERPRETING THE RATIO

When choosing between two results, the IR is a good way to make that decision. A higher ratio means a lower risk for the same return or a higher return for the same risk. A very low, positive ratio means that you gave back all your profits somewhere but finished net ahead. A high ratio, above 1.0 is a pretty smooth upward-trending return. A very high ratio, above 3.0, is probably a sign that you've made an error, did not add costs, or looked ahead at tomorrow's data.

We often search for errors when results are bad, but tend to believe very good answers, even though they are just as likely to be wrong. We just can't help wanting those good results to be correct, only we pay for that with money later. You'll want to train yourself to be critical of all results.

NOT EVERYONE USES THE INFORMATION RATIO

While the information ratio is my choice, not everyone favors it. Some prefer the Calmar Ratio, which is the AROR divided by the maximum drawdown. The maximum drawdown, an absolute number, may seem easier to deal with than the probability of a drawdown, which is how the annualized volatility is represented. On the negative side, as we go forward in time, the drawdowns are likely to get bigger, so the Calmar Ratio is likely to understate the future risk.

Some other developers like to use the standard deviation of the drawdowns, measuring each daily drawdown from the peak equity, and then taking the standard deviation of those values. This seems reasonable because drawdowns can be sharper than rallies and some don't recover quickly, so it's a good measurement of only the losing patterns. The argument against it is that upside volatility is also a sign of potential downside risk. If you've created a system with only small drawdowns, the measurement will be deceptive and you'll be in for an unpleasant surprise.

Even with their faults, some way of measuring reward to risk is necessary when comparing two different trading strategies.

NUMBER OF TRADES

There is a strong argument that a large number of trades add confidence to the results. It's called *statistical significance*. If you have only one trade during the past 10 years, it's going to be hard to judge the value of the system. Long-term trend systems may average two or three trades per year in each market, but a short-term strategy may have 50 per year, 500 over 10 years. It's hard to overfit a short-term system with that many trades.

EXPECTATIONS

How close will your actual performance come to the results you've seen in your testing? Not very close if you've picked the highest-performing combination of parameters that were tested. Most likely, it has benefited from very fortunate timing and is not likely to be repeated.

If you've used multiple parameters, properly spaced, to get an average return, then your test results will be much closer to expectations, but it's unlikely to be as good as the system average. I've already mentioned that, over time, new patterns will emerge and that our systems won't handle them as well as patterns that it saw during testing.

As a general rule, expect twice the risk going forward. Note that I didn't say half the return. It's the risk that seems to be the issue. Expect the ratio to drop nearly 50% when you test out-of-sample data. Expect another drop when you look at actual trading results. It's another reason why you should err on the side of caution and don't overleverage your account.

As you get better at development, you should be closing the gap between the systematic (theoretical) results and real trading performance.

CHAPTER 11

Beating It into Submission

There is more to say about dealing with tests that don't produce the results you want. I think about this as a critical point in development, one in which you take the path that gives you the best chance of success, or you overfit the data so that there is no chance that the end product will work.

FIXING LOSING PERIODS

When you get disappointing results, you will look specifically at the trades, or sequence of trades, that caused the loss. Would a different stop-loss help? Were prices too volatile? Did you enter following a trade with a very large profit? Was this a short sale in a rising market? All of these questions seem valid, so why is there a problem?

It all depends on how you view the results based on those changes. For example, it's a problem if:

- The change corrects only one trade.
- The change affects only one market.

- The results of an optimization show higher peak returns using some parameters, but lower returns using other parameters. That is, profits are concentrated in one area at the cost of other areas.
- The new results are unreasonably good.

The third point, changing the pattern of results, needs to be clear. Consider the test results shown in Figure 11.1. The original test results are the dark line, going from negative 1,000, presumably the shortest calculation period, to 1,425 at the peak, and down to 1,100 at the right, the slowest period. Note that the results flatten out on the right because the percentage difference in the calculation periods get smaller and the results are similar.

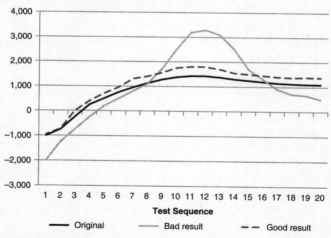

FIGURE 11.1 Test Results Shown after Changes That Cause Concentration of Profits in the Center Compared to Changes That Improve All Test Results

After the rules are changed to improve some specific problems, the new test, shown by the gray line, results in much higher peak profits, while the wings of the results are worse than the original test. You may like this solution at first, but the concentration of improvement shows that a particular situation was targeted. This pattern can be found by quants using kurtosis, which essentially measures the peak. Normal kurtosis has the value of 3 (the shape of a standard bell curve), and anything above 6 is seen as a very narrow peak in the center and should be considered a problem.

By contrast, the "good" result shown in Figure 11.1 as a broken line improves most results in a more uniform manner. This is the ideal result, a change of rules that even improves the worst test results. A rule that achieves this result will be generalized, that is, it won't focus on a particular trade, but on the nature of price movements. We'll discuss this more in the sections that follow.

USE THE AVERAGE RESULTS

My own way of assessing success may not be attractive to many other traders, but I've never found a reason to do it differently. It requires that you first define the range of parameters that should work for your new strategy.

For example, if you are looking for the long-term trend, then calculation periods from 40 to 120, or 60 to 250, may be ranges that should work. If you are looking at a divergence pattern with a holding period of 3 to 8 days, then the pattern should be formed over 5 to 15 days. If you have an intraday breakout and a holding period of 3 days, then your profit targets should be in the range of 0.50 to 3.50 ATRs. You should *not* choose a wide range with the idea of looking at where the profits lie, then narrowing it down to include only the profitable area.

By defining the range in advance, you validate your idea of what works. If only 25% of the tests in your range turn out to be profitable, you need to rethink why you were wrong. The strategy is not doing what you expected.

Normally, you'll be correct about the choice of the parameter test range and the results will look pretty good. The most important value will be the average of all tests, whether it's net profits or the information ratio. The average result is also the most likely expected return in the future, much like economists forecast the mean (the average) one period ahead. The average is always the safest forecast.

The reasoning behind using the average is that we have a poor record of choosing a single parameter value from the test results that will perform each month going forward in exactly the way it did in the past. The results shown in a 10-year test may be the best net profit, but the way it got there might be erratic, with a sequence of losing months before a profitable run came along.

Consider the best result in a series of 100 tests. What is the likelihood that those parameters will give you the best result in the next month or year? I would argue that the best result is normally the least likely to perform well because it benefited from some unusual price movement, perhaps one or more price shocks. Given enough tests, one test is likely to be on the right side of the market when a surprise event drives prices sharply up or down. That event is not going to be repeated, so basing your parameter selection on an outlier will result in disappointing future performance.

Because I have never been successful at figuring out which specific parameters will perform best in the next month, I try to duplicate the average performance. That's why I measure success by the average of all tests. To get an average result, you need to trade your strategy with a sample of different parameters, but no fewer than three, spread across the whole set of results. If we're looking at a simple moving average method, I usually double the calculation period, for example, 30, 60, and 120 days. The percentage difference gives a better distribution. Then you trade each of the three subsystems with equal amounts. The more subsystems, the closer you get to the average.

Granted, the average result isn't as glamorous as the best results from your tests, but they are more realistic. One of the goals of system development is to accurately predict both the returns and the risk of real trading. I think this approach comes close.

SQUEEZING THE LIFE OUT OF A SYSTEM

One of my favorite short-term systems is the 3-Day Trade. It's not actually three days, but it has a 3-day setup period. The rules for a sell signal go as follows:

- Prices close up two days in a row.
- Sell the next open if higher than today's close or sell the next close if it's higher than today's close.
- Exit on the close of the following day.

It takes three days to trigger the entry and the trade is held for two days if you enter on the open and one day if you enter on the close. The rules are symmetric, so that you buy after two lower closes and a lower open or lower close. In the spirit of improvement, we also can add the rules:

- Take profits if prices move 2 ATRs from the entry.
- Enter short sales any time that prices spike 2.5 ATRs and the price closes in the upper 25% of the daily range.

Both additional rules are generalized based on volatility, so they qualify according to our guidelines, which are discussed more in the next section. The first extra rule, taking profits, will capture any fast, large, and favorable moves in our direction. When we operate in the short-term arena, we expect a lot of market noise, so capturing a profit based on some news announcement will be to our advantage.

The second rule, entering on a price spike without waiting for the 2-day setup, is also reacting to market noise. This rule works best for equity index markets, which tend to have more noise than other sectors. A volatility of 2.5 times the normal volatility is a noticeably strong or weak day, and prices closing near the top or bottom of that range provides the opportunity for a reversal the next day.

Both rules improve results in general over a wide selection of equity index markets and sufficient data. So far, so good.

But there is more. Floor traders have always believed that, during a trend, say an upward move, prices will open higher on Monday, then reverse Tuesday or Wednesday.

Fridays may see selling pressure when some traders exit their positions to go home flat on the weekend. So the days of the week may be important.

Finding out if this pattern is true doesn't require a change of rules, just a way of adding the returns for long and short sales by the day of the week. Using the original rules, plus the two extra ones, we can test three of the primary equity index futures markets, the *e*mini S&P, NASDAQ, and the small caps, the Russell 2000. Figure 11.2 shows the profits and losses by day of the week from 1990 through May 2015.

The results show that Monday is consistently good for buying all three index futures. Mondays and Tuesdays are good for the S&P, and Monday, Tuesday, and Wednesday are excellent for the Russell. Friday is also good for selling the S&P and NQ. Those results seem to confirm the patterns expressed by the floor traders.

LONG TRADES

	Mon	Tue	Wed	Thu	Fri
S&P	485062	357327	−150580	28873	−78595
NQ	67469	−75556	34523	50195	−171604
RU	59712	255387	512269	−46304	−499171

SHORT SALES

	Mon	Tue	Wed	Thu	Fri
S&P	−112991	−18266	−94722	−93925	30641
NQ	−88261	−39942	75661	−185758	94043
RU	68057	−271811	2058	−86041	−342346

FIGURE 11.2   Results by Day of the Week from 1990 for the S&P, NASDAQ, and Russell 2000 Futures

But this isn't the whole picture. Let's look at a more recent period, one year, starting in May 2014, shown in Figure 11.3. While Monday was consistently good for the entire period from 1990, it lost money during the past year. However, Tuesdays were consistently successful for both long and short positions. Thursdays are now very good for the S&P and NQ, even better than the longer test, but the best short sales have changed completely, shifting from Friday to Thursday.

If we look further into the pattern of returns for the past 3 and 5 years, we find that there is even more of a shift. There is no consistency in returns based on the day of the week, but we would not have known that unless we looked deeper into the test results.

The good news is that the results show net profits if you add all the days of the week and avoid short sales. That should not be a surprise because the stock market is biased to the long side.

Rewrite section

		LONG TRADES			
	PLLday1	PLLday2	PLLday3	PLLday4	PLLday5
ES	−13178	41374	20175	21059	−17056
NQ	−11114	47178	−43917	52393	−12270
TO2	−1998	36696	−13698	−28072	3324
		SHORT SALES			
	PLLday1	PLLday2	PLLday3	PLLday4	PLLday5
ES	−13178	41374	20175	21059	−17056
NQ	−11114	47178	−43917	52393	−12270
TO2	−1998	36696	−13698	−28072	3324

FIGURE 11.3 Results by Day from May 2014 for the S&P, NASDAQ, and Russell 2000 Futures.

The lesson to be learned is that a system can be good, but you cannot try to isolate its profitable or losing patterns with too much accuracy. We win because, in the big picture, the numbers are on our side.

GENERALIZING THE RULES

There are a number of techniques that work across both time and markets. They may improve the performance of a wide range of systems. The most important of these are based on volatility.

Volatility is measured by the equities industry as the standard deviation of the daily returns times the square root of 252. There is an example of that in Chapter 9. But a better measure is the average true range, also discussed in Chapter 9.

High Volatility

High volatility is associated with high risk, but many traders think that their systems perform better during periods of high volatility. For certain, nothing does well when prices aren't moving, and arbitrage programs will benefit from larger per share returns when volatility causes the two legs to go farther apart. But is that the real benefit?

In many cases, the payout for identifying high volatility is the ability to reduce the risk. We know that high volatility is the same as high risk, but we don't know that it will also result in high returns. In fact, it is not likely, especially for trend following. For trades taken when the volatility is high, we see higher risk but not necessarily higher returns. That translates into a lower information ratio, which is the way we measure a successful strategy.

For short-term traders, I find that annualized volatility over 45% to 50% is too high. It is easy to skip those trades because there are always more to come. For long-term traders, I would look at reducing your exposure. Most often, that's the same as taking profits, then resetting when volatility returns to near normal.

We'll look at this again in Chapter 13.

Low Volatility

Low volatility is more complex. Markets can be lethargic at low volatility, meandering up and down, not going anywhere. In commodities in which a low price in wheat or metals can mean that it is trading near the level of production costs, there may be an exodus of traders looking for something more exciting. Lower liquidity and unchanged fundamentals will result in sideways price moves at the same time as low volatility. In general, a market that has low volatility is a poor place to put your money, no matter what your strategy is.

But there is another important aspect of low volatility. For some markets, such as interest rates, it could mean a steady move in one direction. While the relationship of return to risk is very good, the returns are very small. For futures traders, especially hedge funds using macrotrend systems, those periods are usually leveraged up so that the returns are larger, even though risk is also higher. Without leveraging up, results would never achieve expectations.

CHAPTER 12

More on Futures

I started in this business trading futures. At that time, there were only commodities, agricultural products and metals; not even energy. When my orders in grains got big enough, I was able to go on the floor with my broker. It was exciting. I would give him a price to buy a million soybeans and he would run into the pit, wave his arms, and come back out saying, "Filled." I saw it as the ultimate in free trade.

One day, all the grain markets were limit up. That's when prices have gone as far as allowed in one day. In this case, it was an unexpectedly bullish crop report. Very little happens at limit up and the floor was remarkably quiet, just a few contracts trading hands at the limit price every few minutes. I was just thinking of leaving because nothing was happening.

Before I say more, let me describe the layout of the trading floor at the Chicago Board of Trade. I'm in the back left corner of a very large room at the soybean pit. To the far left are two wide doors, one in each corner. So the farthest door is diagonally across from me, the farthest point in the room. The trading pits all line the outside of the room, and are different sizes based on the activity of that commodity. Corn is the biggest, soybeans the next largest. Gold, destined for failure, was small.

Having just made my decision to leave for lunch, there was a murmur at the pit farthest from me, near one of the doors. The murmur got quickly louder. My broker's ears were standing up. "There's some news." The news must be negative for prices, given the rising volume of sound across the floor. Traders must be selling.

The volume of yelling moved to the left, counterclockwise around the room, embroiling the next pit. It reached the corner to my left. My broker said, "Something is wrong. We'd better get out of our position." I nodded and he ran into the pit, hands facing out, selling at the market before it collapsed. He returned looking pleased.

Just then, a streaker ran by. For those not familiar with the early 1970s, a streaker is a hippie version of Lady Godiva.

"Oh, no," my broker yelled (maybe not quite those exact words), and ran back into the pit to buy back our position. Too late. Soybeans were back to limit up with a pool of buy orders waiting.

The moral of the story is to follow your system. Floor brokers do well, but they have a very short time frame. A few hours is a long-term trade for them, and getting out first has served them well as risk management, but it doesn't work as well for us.

LEVERAGE

The biggest difference between trading commodities compared to stocks is the leverage. With stocks you normally buy the shares at the full price, which means there is no leverage. You could borrow some of the money, often up to 50%, which will give you leverage of 2:1, less the cost of financing.

Commodities are completely different. *Margin* in commodities is a good faith deposit, not the amount borrowed. In general, you can estimate the amount needed to trade at 10% of the face value of the commodity contract, more for equity index, less for agricultural commodities. Exact rates are provided by your broker. Some brokers allow you to put up securities, such as T-bills, for most of the margin. So unlike stock margin, where you pay, with futures margin you might earn interest.

If your margin averages 10%, then your initial leverage is 10:1. I say "initial" because, if you lose 25% of the margin, you must replace that money. That's called *maintenance margin*. The best practice is to use only about 40% of your investment for margin and leave the rest as reserve. Then the 10:1 leverage becomes 4:1 and you don't need to worry about maintenance margin because your reserves will cover any drawdowns.

With 4:1 leverage, all the price moves are essentially multiplied by four, just the way a leveraged ETF can be two or three times the return. To put this in perspective, Long-Term Capital Management was able to leverage their trading to 50:1. That will keep you up at night.

CONVERSION FACTORS FOR CALCULATING RETURNS

Unlike stocks, where your profit or loss for the day is the change in price times the number of shares, futures need another multiplier, what we call the *conversion factor*. It's the value of one *big point* move in price, where a big point is the number to the left of the decimal.

For example, corn is priced in quarters of a cent per bushel, so a price of 325.75 means $3.2575 per bushel. One big point is equal to one cent. Because most grain contracts are 5,000 bushels, the value of a one-cent move is $50. That's also the conversion factor. You can find the value of one big point move on the exchange website (www.cmegroup.com) under *contract specifications*. Therefore, if you owned two contracts of corn, and the price moved 2½ cents yesterday, you would have made 50 × 2.5 × 2 (contracts) = $250. With the margin on corn now at $1,000, you can buy 5,000 bushels for May delivery at $3.60, for a value of $18,000. A gain of $250 would be about 1.4% if you treated margin as the investment. But it's not.

The best way to calculate returns on any one commodity, or stock, is to divide the current profit by your full investment. If you were trading 10 different commodities or stocks with an investment of $50,000, then your return would be 250/50,000 = 5 basis points, or 5/100ths of a percent for corn. Hopefully, you are trading other markets at the same time, which will add up to larger returns.

DON'T FORGET FX

Futures are international. If you're trading interest rates or equity index markets, you'll want to include both the United States and Europe. For trend followers, Europe tends to be better than the United States and for mean reversion systems, the U.S. index markets are preferable because they're noisier.

One interesting strategy is to arbitrage the movement between the U.S. 10-year note and the Eurobund, also a maturity of about 10 years. First, make sure that you are trading while both markets are open. If you're testing the strategy, you'll need to capture data at the same time of day. The European primary day session closes at about 11:30 New York time, so for daily data, you need a series of 10-year note prices at 11:30 to use along with the close of the European market. Be sure your data for Europe is not the "extended session," which ends at the same time as the U.S. market but is less liquid at that time. Four in the afternoon in New York is 10 P.M. in Germany and most traders have gone home for the night. That may be convenient because the U.S. and EUREX closes are the same time, but you might not be happy with the fills.

FX QUOTES

Futures prices are always quoted in the local currency. A move in the Eurobund might be a quarter of a point, or from 159.00 to 159.25. The contract size is €100,000, and the conversion factor is €1,000. For one contract, that move is a profit or loss of €250. Note everything is in euros, just as all U.S. markets are in dollars.

If you're a U.S. trader, then you'll want to convert the returns from all foreign markets into U.S. dollars. If you're in France, you'll want them all in euros. No problem. Just multiply the returns from the Eurobund by the value of the

EURUSD cash exchange rate, now at about 1.08. A gain of €250 becomes $270. We'll ignore any cost of conversion, although there may be some small difference in the exchange rates to include costs.

Trading around the world requires that you convert all the returns to USD, or your own currency, each day. If you want everything in USD, the exchange rate should always reflect "how many U.S. dollars you get for each foreign currency unit." That's expressed by having the USD second in the currency designation. So the Swiss franc, CHFUSD, is USD per CHF. But the CHF is one of those currencies that the traders have always quoted as USD-CHF (called the "dollar-Swiss," so you need to change it to CHFUSD = 1/USDCHF. It's not hard, but you don't want to forget.

The major currencies (the "big 8") that are quoted "normally" are the euro (EURUSD), Australian dollar (AUDUSD), and British pound (GBPUSD). Currencies that tend to be quoted "backward," by convention, are the Swiss franc (USDCHF), Japanese yen (USDJPY), and Canadian dollar (USDCAD). The other two majors are the EURJPY and the EURGBP. Hong Kong and Singapore are also quoted as the inverse. It's important to understand how the exchange rates are quoted before you trade outside your own country. Some data services quote them differently. Bloomberg, for example, doesn't tell you how it's quoted. You just need to know by the price. On April 29, 2015, the euro was posted as 1.1124, which would be EURUSD (dollars per euro), while the Mexican peso was 15.21, USDMXN (pesos per dollar).

REAL DIVERSIFICATION

In the equities market, I find that equity ETFs seem highly correlated, that is, most tend to move the same way on the same day. Specific stocks can be different. Even while the S&P index is moving higher, some stocks can be heading straight down. Trying to create a stock portfolio of individual securities that are both fundamentally different and less correlated in their price moves is going to be very difficult. If you're going to make money from the price going higher, then the very fact that they are moving higher at the same time will make them more correlated.

There is also the arbitrage of the S&P cash index with the S&P futures. When those two markets diverge to a level that can be profitable for arbitrageurs, they will buy all the stocks in the S&P and sell the futures (when the cash index is at a discount to the futures), bringing them back into line. They also cause all the stocks to move in a correlated way.

Futures offer a different type of diversification. Futures markets tend to be grouped into six sectors: interest rates, forex, equity index, energy, metals, and agricultural. Sometimes the interest rates are separated into long and short maturities, metals into precious and nonferrous, and agricultural is separated into grains, livestock, and softs (cocoa, sugar, coffee, and sometimes cotton).

The interrelationship of commodity markets can be complex. Interest rate moves permeate everything because they define the cost of carry in all commodities. After all, nothing is free. If you own a contract of gold for delivery six months ahead, you are paying the cost of carrying that gold (the interest on the total value of the contract plus storage and insurance) for six months. If the cost of soybeans rises, the cost of feeding livestock rises as well. If the U.S. dollar declines in value, wheat will rise to adjust to the export value in another currency.

Looking past the macroeconomic factors, there is a real difference between the price movement of copper and that of wheat. There is no arbitrage that says, "If copper is at $2.50 per pound, then wheat should be at $5 per bushel." However, I do remember the saying, "An ounce of silver buys a pound of meat."

You don't need any math to group futures into the obvious six sectors. You need to be aware that not all sectors offer good diversification. Interest rates are highly correlated, that is, when the U.S. raises rates, it's likely that other countries will follow. Although the Fed may raise rates to dampen inflation, it's also a way to strengthen the dollar. Higher rates attract investors from all over the world. They need to buy U.S. dollars before they can buy the 10-year note. To avoid all money flowing into the United States, other countries will need to raise their rates to compete.

Other commodity sectors are not as correlated. Metals include both gold and copper. While gold is used as a hedge against inflation, copper is used in housing. They are fundamentally unrelated. Corn and coffee, both agricultural products, are unrelated. Even crude oil and natural gas are only occasionally related by some severe economic event.

When you trade a portfolio of futures markets, be sure that you choose equal exposure across at least three sectors. You can read more about this in Chapter 13.

THE LIFE CYCLE OF A COMMODITY MARKET

Stocks disappear and so do commodities. The Live Hog contract is now the Lean Hog contract. I'm still wondering what a "lean hog" is. The Pork Bellies contract, the basis for bacon, has gone out of vogue after once being the favorite of traders.

Figure 12.1 shows the volume of orange juice futures. Volume has been declining for the past three years. Are our children drinking less orange juice? Is the price too high? Yes, the price is too high, but there are other factors.

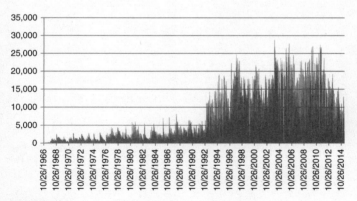

FIGURE 12.1   Volume of Orange Juice Futures (in contracts)

Consumers have more choices for drinks, not all of them healthy, but any choice dilutes the rest of the market. And speaking of diluting, the consumers are moving away from "frozen concentrated orange juice" to fresh juice, that is, those who aren't drinking soda and energy-enhanced drinks.

This is just a "heads up" that markets change and liquidity disappears. Be careful to monitor both the stocks and futures markets that you trade. Not that we expect today's Apple to be tomorrow's Radio Shack, but it's good to remember that Apple was once nearly out of business.

CHAPTER 13

I Don't Want No Stinkin' Risk

Most of us would rather discuss profits than risk. Have you noticed that the financial news on television is filled with people discussing how high a stock will go and not how much risk it has? Wouldn't you be more willing to tune in to a show that was explaining why gold will go to $2,000 by the end of the year, and not to someone discussing the chance of Apple losing 25% of its value?

Risk is just not as exciting as trying to make the big hit. You want to know if you should buy oil at $50 before it goes back to $90 or $120. Of course, that's a mistake because you can't capture the big profit without knowing the risk. The talking heads on television continue to say that, "If you had held your positions through the 2008 financial crisis, you would have made it all back, and more." Right. But not many people did that because, when you see your retirement account drop to half its value, or more, you want out before it goes to zero. That's what happens in a financial crisis—people panic. In truth, it's difficult to be rational when prices have dropped by 50%.

In early 2000 when the Internet bubble peaked, there were a lot of traders who entered NASDAQ stocks late in the 1990s because it seemed as though prices would never stop going up (see Figure 13.1). When the decline started, many, if not most, financial advisers said, "Stay with it, it's just a correction." When the index had dropped 50%, they said, "We expect prices to stabilize here." By April 2001, the NASDAQ had moved below 1,500. "Why get out now, we must be near the bottom?" Finally, in August 2002, NASDAQ had lost 85% of its value. What responsible investment advice or financial planning could allow you to hold those positions through an 85% decline? That's not risk management, that's wishful thinking. And that's unprofessional.

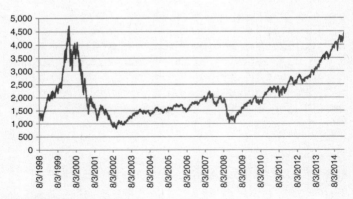

FIGURE 13.1　NASDAQ 100 (NDX) Index

A CLEAR PLAN

As an argument in favor of trend following, nearly any long-term trend would have gotten you out of the market in 2000 or 2008, with a modest loss and kept you out for the remainder of the decline. But that's not the point right now. The point is that we need risk controls and they must be followed. It's not the everyday risks that are the problem, we do it because of the rare exceptions.

Crisis alpha is a new term that expresses the way futures performance diversifies a typical stock portfolio. It shows that futures may not keep up with equity returns in many of the years, but they show outstanding returns during a crisis when stocks plummet.

In Chapter 9, *Equal Opportunity Trading*, we discussed the basics of risk. Let me summarize them:

1. Start every trade with the same risk.
2. System diversification is better than market diversification.
3. Try to make all levels of risk equal, if liquidity is not a problem.
4. Avoid low-priced stocks because they behave erratically.
5. Have a risk management plan. Nearly any trading system will have built-in risk controls.

Because it's so important, let me repeat, "If you put more risk on any one trade, then that trade must have proportionately bigger returns." If you can do that, great. I can't.

AVOID LOW-PRICED STOCKS

There is some truth to the common thinking that the best risk management is simply to avoid the risk. Understanding the basics of volatility is one way to do that.

Low-priced stocks turn out to be less profitable for most trading systems. Figure 13.2 shows Bank of America (BAC), a prime candidate in the 2008 financial crisis. The stock price is gray and uses the left scale; the annualized volatility is black and uses the right scale. It's easy to see that volatility spiked in 2008 while prices fell. It did that again in late 2011. Also notice the period between the crises, 2003 to 2007, when prices rose and volatility fell, as is also the case since 2012. From my point of view, low prices *and* high volatility are to be avoided. There are better opportunities.

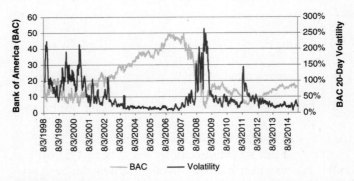

FIGURE 13.2 Bank of America Price and Volatility, including the Financial Crisis of 2008

When prices are low and volatility is low, daily returns are small. For a short-term trader, that means struggling to offset costs. For a trend follower, it means days of under-performing your expectations.

Just to give price movement a bit more dimension, volatility as a percentage of price actually decreases as prices increase. In absolute terms, volatility does increase. A stock may trade in a range of $0.50 at $10 and $4.00 at $100, a larger range in dollars but a smaller range in percent. The danger comes at very low price levels, when a stock, such as Bank of America, has sold off to an unreasonable low price (which we know after the fact). It can post volatility of 2, 3, or even 5 times the amount that it showed in previous times under normal conditions. Mixing very high and very low price stocks in your portfolio can produce an unbalanced effect.

VOLATILITY OVER 100%?

The right scale on the BAC chart shows the annualized volatility topping 250%. Of course, that's not possible. It's caused by using only 20 days of price returns and then extrapolating that for a full year. It's not technically an error, only confusing, but that's the industry standard, so we all use it. It's consistent in its own way and it's the same formula used for options implied volatility. You can still use those numbers to decide when it's too risky to trade. Just remember that it's not the actual volatility.

DON'T TRADE WHEN VOLATILITY IS VERY HIGH

The BAC chart lets me say that I don't trade when volatility is very high, and I don't recommend that you do. For me, "high" is around 50%, using the 20-day calculation period. For BAC, that's low on the chart, the first horizontal line above zero. It's not that you can't make money when volatility is high; it's just that it's not worth the risk. You don't make extremely high returns when volatility is high, but you do have extremely high risk, so your payout is bad. High volatility can be scary. It's not as predictable as I would like and you need to reduce your trading size drastically. It's easier and safer not to trade at those times.

SIDESTEPPING PRICE SHOCKS

Yes, I'm really kidding. You can't sidestep price shocks because we have no idea when they will happen. You can, however, lower the chances that you will be caught by being in the market less time.

If you have a choice of two trading strategies, one that is in the market all the time (such as macrotrend trading), and a short-term method that's in the market only 15% of the time, then the short-term method has an 85% less chance of being hit with a price shock. It may even have a lower chance because a price shock will very often move against a trend position, which represents the general direction the public is holding, while a short-term method may be on either side of the market and not in the direction of the trend. It has a better chance of benefiting from the shock. So, for a short-term system, the 15% chance of taking a loss from a price shock may be closer to 7.5% while a trend system will remain near 100%.

PORTFOLIO DRAWDOWN

When we decide to trade, we have an expectation of our maximum drawdown based on some historical testing or analysis. If we're a passive stock trader, we judge drawdowns by looking at the price swings, and if we're a systematic trader, we use the return stream. With futures, we decide on the leverage based on the maximum drawdown that we expect.

There are three big concerns:

1. Did you pick parameters that unrealistically minimized historical drawdowns?

   Hopefully, we've dealt with that earlier and you're using multiple parameters, including realistic costs, tested enough data, and done most everything else right that is within your control.

2. Even if your testing is correct, price swings, profits, and losses all get bigger over time.

   The more data you accumulate, the greater the chance of a longer run of profits and losses. It's the same with flipping a coin. With 64 flips (sorry about the odd number but it needs to be a power of 2), you can expect only one run of 4 heads or tails. With 128 flips, you can expect a run of 5. Each time you double the number of flips, you can expect a run of one more.

As time goes by, more days are added to your flips and the chances of larger profits and losses increase. It's all in the numbers.

3. No matter what maximum risk you plan for, there is always a chance that you'll be staring at the largest loss you are willing to take. What do you do?

You've tested your strategy over 10 years. Given the normal volatility of the stock market and a reasonable portfolio mix, you have a 16% chance of losing 12% over 10 years, as well as other drawdowns of varying amounts. That doesn't sound so bad. But you also have a 2.5% chance of losing 24% over the same period, and less than a 1% chance of losing 36%. Given enough time, it will happen. But your risk management rule says that you can't lose more than 20% or you need to quit. Professional managers face this problem all the time because their clients want higher returns but not the risk that goes with it, so they put an artificial risk limit on the account.

BUSINESS RISK

We call this last point *business risk* because it's not the system but a constraint that you accept because you want to have that client, or you want bigger returns and will hope that the risk doesn't show up until after you've captured the profit. Which can happen. It's similar to the choice gamblers make when they double down and hope that the long run doesn't come in the first 50% of the play. If they're right, they take their profit and move to another table, or quit (less likely).

What do you do when your cut-off is 20% and you're down 15%? Do you keep trading the same way, double down, or scale back? Given the small but realistic chance that losses will continue, doubling down is very risky. If you're a professional manager, you risk your client's money and your business if you're wrong. I don't think that's a good option.

Trading at the same leverage is less of a risk, but still a fairly high risk. Probabilities say that you will exceed the maximum loss from time to time. Can you take the chance that this is one of those times?

That leaves us with only one option: scaling down our position size and consequently our leverage, so that we reduce any future losses. At the same time, it makes it more difficult to recover those losses. That's the rub. You save the account but may underperform your peers when the performance recovers.

Personally, I don't see that there is much choice. By deleveraging, you reduce the chance of reaching the maximum drawdown, which is good for both your client and your business. I have found that scaling back when we get between ½ and ⅔ of the maximum loss is a good place. You can start reducing your positions in 15% or 20% increments, eventually getting to a leverage of only 15% of the original amount. We hope it never gets there, but if it did, you've saved the account.

GEARING BACK UP

The leveraging down part is pretty straightforward. You scale down equally as the account reaches new lows. The real problem comes in scaling back up. First understand that there is no way you can do this without giving up profits when the system starts to perform again. You can't just put back all the positions on the first day the system has a profit. As far as I know, there is no automatic, clever way to do it, but I'll give you my best solution.

You've lost 15% out of a maximum of 20% allowed by your risk management rule. Your leverage is now at, say, 25% of the original investment. You need to put back 75%. Follow these rules:

- Wait for profits to recover by 5% of the original, fully leveraged portfolio.
- Then wait for a loss (another retracement) of about 2% ($\frac{2}{5}$ of the gain).
- Add 10% to 20% of the leverage back.

The reason for waiting for a pullback is that you can't afford to add back leverage and see another drawdown right away. If you are more aggressive, you don't need to wait for the pullback, but if the program loses money again, then you will need to deleverage sooner. Leveraging up and leveraging down too often makes you look uncertain.

CHAPTER 14

Picking the Best Stocks (and Futures Markets) for Your Portfolio

I wish it wasn't so, but I don't have enough capital to trade all of the stocks in the S&P 500 using my strategies. I need to select stocks that will outperform the average, hopefully by quite a bit. I've heard this called "smart beta," which is also "alpha." So we're adding considerable value if we can do this right.

ASKING TOO MUCH

We keep coming back to realistic expectations. Some years ago I spent considerable time developing a classic portfolio allocation program, more or less based on Markowitz's mean-variance approach. In that method, you found the optimal portfolio based on risk, reward, and correlation. That method was the industry benchmark for years. We won't discuss it because there is no proof that I've found that says it has any predictive value. It simply finds the best combination based on past data. We'd like something that actually does better than the market index in real trading.

Being skillful at programming and math, I decided that the best portfolio was not only the one with an excellent return, but one that varied the least from the steady upward progress of returns. Another way of saying that is I wanted the returns to look as close as possible to a straight line going up.

As it turns out, with enough manipulation of data, weighting the trades to emphasize the winning ones and avoiding those that have large equity swings, you can get a very impressive result. Unfortunately, when I started trading that portfolio, or at least monitoring the performance out of sample, it was horrible. It was a lesson in trying to force returns into something that it was not. It is not possible to either predict or structure a portfolio, or even a trading system, in a way that you control. The market has a mind of its own and you need to understand that it will refuse to fit your agenda.

At the very beginning of this book, I emphasized that the solution was well-described by the phrase "loose pants fit everyone." That goes for specifying a strategy and also for a portfolio.

THE PRACTICAL SOLUTION

You have $100,000 to invest in the stock market, and you've worked out a good strategy. There are hundreds of actively traded stocks and you want to choose the best 10 for your portfolio. How do you do that? It's not as difficult as you might think because, as we've seen in other chapters, a simple method can be better than a complex one.

As it turns out, we can rank stocks and futures markets by performance based on a specific strategy. For example, interest rates tend to be best for trend systems and equity index for mean reversion. Of course, that doesn't mean they're best every day. During 2008, and especially in 2012, interest rates were the big losers in macrotrend portfolios, even more so because they were a disproportionally large part of institutional portfolios.

Figure 14.1 shows the NAV of the interest rate and equity index sectors for a well-diversified futures portfolio of U.S. and European markets. After 2008, the steady climb of both sectors changed to erratic and sideways performance. Without seeking markets that had the potential for better returns, institutions would suffer a prolonged period of underperformance. In the second chart, Figure 14.2, we can see that the erratic NAV of the PIMCO Total Return Fund (PPTRX) has resulted in about 40% redemptions (source: www.investments.pimco.com).

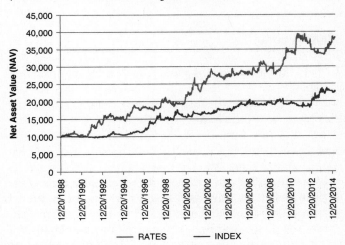

FIGURE 14.1 Returns of a Trend Portfolio of U.S. and EU Futures

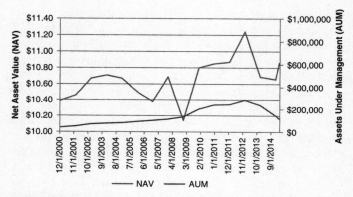

FIGURE 14.2 PIMCO Total Return Fund (PPTRX) Showing the Net Asset Value (NAV) and the Assets under Management (AUM)

RANKING SUCCESS

To avoid the problems of PIMCO and underperformance in general, we need to be able to select markets for our portfolio that have the best chance for success. We can't look back too far because we would never see the way some stocks or futures markets rotate from trending to nontrending and from bad to good performance. What seems to make sense is to say that a market should be profitable on a strategy for approximately the past two years, to show that it actually works with the strategy. It doesn't matter if it made a lot or a little, just that it was profitable.

In the first step, we eliminate all markets that lost money during the past two years. Using the remaining markets, we now rank their performance over a shorter time frame, say three months. Finally, we select from the top down to fill the portfolio.

Note that we used only profits for ranking. What about an information ratio, the returns divided by the risk? That way, we would not only get a good return, but a small risk. How nice! But why stop there? Let's look for returns that were very, very smooth, with no downward plunges in equity at all. At this point it should be clear that we're asking too much. If we constrain our choice by too many conditions, our efforts to select the best markets will fail. It's identical to overfitting trading rules. You can't force a market to perform in a certain way or expect it to continue to perform that way. You can only ask for the simplest criterion. Remember "loose pants." So profits seem to be the single best choice, but feel free to try something more complicated.

We can now select a portfolio of only a few stocks that have a good chance of outperforming the broader index. A word of caution, however: Those stocks that outperform usual have higher volatility than the index, so you can expect higher profits on good days and larger losses on bad days. It's not exactly a high beta portfolio, but it's similar.

We can apply this to futures markets in a similar way. Rank futures by performance and take the top ones for your portfolio. Only for futures, you must limit the number of markets you can take from any one sector. That way you don't end up with all your money in interest rates, or any one sector. If it turns out that interest rates is the only sector making money, then you will have a smaller number of markets in your portfolio and lower leverage. It seems better to have fewer markets that are making money than a widely diversified portfolio of markets that are mostly not making money.

ROTATION

You've picked the 10 stocks for the portfolio, but at some point those stocks won't be as good as others. You'll need to rotate them out of the portfolio and replace them with new, better candidates.

The process is simple. Each day you rank a large set of stocks (at least 250) by their system performance. As long as your 10 stocks stay in the upper 15 spots of the ranking, continue to hold those stocks. If one falls to rank 16, replace it with the highest-ranking stock not already in the portfolio.

It may be that the stock that you've removed is still making money, but not as much as one that is higher up in the rank. It does sound like overfitting, doesn't it? But it seems to be the latest in portfolio technology and is remarkably simple, which is the main reason why it works.

You can prove it to yourself, as I have, by creating a portfolio of 10 stocks and calculating the historical performance. Then reduce that number to eight. The performance should get better because you are using higher-ranked stocks. It may also get more volatile because you have fewer stocks. You can also try to reduce the buffer zone (the 5 extra positions before you remove a stock) to 4 or 3, remembering that you'll be switching more often. Or, you can increase the size of the zone and hold the stocks longer. It's always best to learn as much as you can about your trading program. It will give you confidence to use it.

CHAPTER 15

Matching the Strategy to the Market

Much earlier in this book, I referred to the *efficiency ratio* as a way of measuring price noise. In turn, lower noise means that prices are moving smoothly. "Smoothly" does not say anything about the volatility, only that the price is going consistently in one direction. When the direction changes, it goes consistently in the new direction. Low noise is good for trend following; high noise is good for mean reversion. In this chapter, we look at how some of the markets are ranked. In that way, you can decide which markets are more likely to be successful with your strategy.

We can define the efficiency ratio as the net change in price over *n* days divided by the sum of the absolute changes over the same period. Then, if the market goes from one price to another in a straight line, it is highly efficient (actually, perfectly efficient) and best exploited with a directional approach, such as trend following. If prices move up and down, much like a drunken sailor's walk, it is inefficient, the ratio is low, and a mean reversion approach is best.

Applying the efficiency ratio to futures, and even ETFs, is more accurate than applying it to individual stocks. A single stock can change its character based on news, the resignation of the CEO, an announcement that they've lost a lot of money in a foreign exchange hedge, or other unique events, but an index or highly liquid futures market maintains the same type of price movements for long periods of time.

NOISE FOR STOCKS

You may want to decide on the nature of the specific market based on your own observations, but the following might help. First is a chart of selected stocks (Figure 15.1), sorted by highest ratio (strongest trend) to lowest ratio values. Note that the high-tech stocks are on the left, indicating the strongest trends, and the established old companies, Exxon Mobil (XOM), American Express (AXP), and Wal-Mart (WMT) are on the right, indicating either no big trends or a lot of backing and filling. Overall, using the noise measurement seems to sort them correctly.

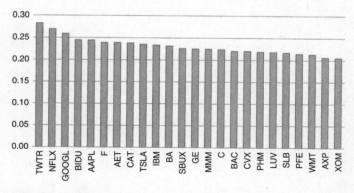

FIGURE 15.1 Selected Stocks Sorted by Noise Ratio

Can we see the difference between NFLX and XOM on a price chart? It's not easy because noise is measuring the average efficiency of each 20-day period. Figure 15.2 shows NFLX and XOM, two extremes. It's not the long period of small movement that makes NFLX a trending market, but the more recent bursts of strength and weakness. The XOM price movements have many more alternating up and down days.

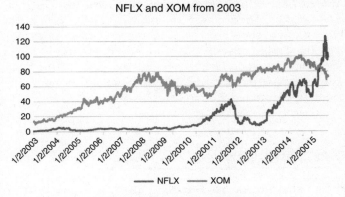

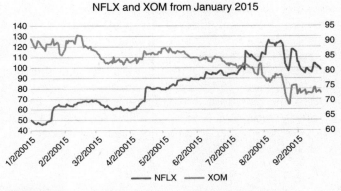

FIGURE 15.2 Comparing NFLX and XOM, Two Noise Extremes, Visually

NOISE FOR ETFs

As for ETFs, the most liquid are subsets of stocks, which are themselves noisy, so most ETFs are also noisy. However, there is another factor that enters into the level of noise for each market, and that is the trading activity and the nature of the participants. An inactive market, or a newly traded one, is likely to be dominated by a few commercial interests. These players often have the same opinion of where prices should be heading and will cause unusually sustained price moves on low volume. That results in a high efficiency ratio and favors trend following. Be on the lookout for those markets because they present an unusually good opportunity for short-term profits.

NOISE FOR FUTURES

I find the futures markets the most interesting because they span the range of equities, foreign exchange, interest rates, and commodities. Some of these have explosive moves. Figure 15.3 gives a much broader perspective than stocks. On the left are mostly short-term interest rate markets, which track Central Bank policy. On the right are many equity index markets, most with very broad investor participation. Note that the S&P is much farther to the right than NASDAQ, indicating that NASDAQ tends to have wider price swings, making it somewhat less noisy.

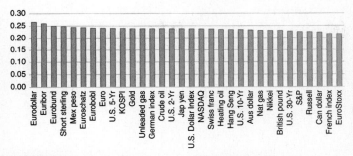

FIGURE 15.3 Average Noise for Selected Futures Markets

The conclusion is that, for most trading strategies, we would want to go in the direction of the breakout for the short-term interest rates, and fade the move for the equity index markets, that is, sell an upward breakout and buy a downward breakout.

CHAPTER 16

Constructing a Trend Strategy

We've discussed a lot of issues needed to create a sound algorithmic trading strategy, but it's necessary to put it all together to solidify those ideas. If you've decided to base the strategy on a long-term trend, there are still a number of specific decisions to make with regard to the strategy, including:

1. The trending technique.
2. The rules for buying and selling.
3. Stop-loss or other individual trade risk controls.
4. Profit-taking and reentry.
5. Single or multiple entries and exits.

There are also other decisions that apply to any strategy:

a. Position sizing.
b. Volatility filters.
c. The test plan, including the markets to test, the date range over which the strategy should work, and the criteria you'll apply to decide if it's successful.
d. Creating and testing a portfolio of stocks, ETFs, or futures markets.

You could get much more complicated, but if you can work through these points successfully, you will have created a strategy that's likely to succeed.

THE TREND

The concept is that a long-term trend captures the underlying direction of the market, that is, the way prices react to economic policy, and tries to ignore the noise caused by day-to-day news releases. We know that the long-term ("macro") trend has a history of success, and we want to participate. The three most likely candidates for identifying the trend are the moving average, the breakout, and the linear regression.

As we've stated earlier, any one of these can be doing better than the others for short periods of time. In the long run all of them make money when the underlying price trends and none of them are profitable when the market flounders. What differentiates one method from the other is the risk profile.

The *moving average* cuts losses short while looking to capture the long-term move. Generally, only 30% to 35% of the trades are profitable, but the size of the profits is about 2.5 to 3.0 times the size of the losses. Small losses are good, but a sequence of small losses can be a bigger loss, no matter how you total the result.

The *breakout* buys a new high and sells a new low. Its trade risk is the difference between the high and the low. If you use a long-term breakout, say 80 days, then the risk is the difference between the 80-day high and the 80-day low, which could be large. On the other hand, prices can flop around anywhere within that range and you don't get stopped out, so there is a much higher percentage of profitable trades, often about 60%.

Linear regression risk falls somewhere in between, as does its percentage of profitable trades. Its main difference is that it smooths prices using a straight line. When the slope of the line turns up, we buy, and when it turns down, we sell. Some analysts put a band around the line and project it forward one day, then see if prices break through the band. If the trend has been up and prices cross the lower band heading down, we can anticipate the downtrend.

BUYING AND SELLING RULES

To keep it simple, we will buy when the moving average turns up, when the closing price breaks above the previous high, or when the slope of the regression turns up. Of these three, I consider the breakout more responsive because you enter a long when prices a making a new high. There is no lag.

We sell when the opposite occurs, although we don't go short stocks or ETFs, only futures. The bias in the stock market, and the unusual asymmetry of price movement to the upside and downside, make the short sales far less likely to be profitable for a slow trending method. In the next chapter, we'll see that an intraday strategy doesn't have this problem.

FIRST TESTS

At this point, we stop to define the rest of the problem, for which there are two parts:

- What calculation periods should we expect to work?
- What markets should we trade?

To capture the economic direction of prices, you'll need at least two months of data, even three months. At the upper end, using a 250-day trend would remove any seasonal variation, but give us very few trades. Experience has shown that about half of that, or 120 days, is the longest calculation period that's practical. Then, when we test, we want to cover the range from about 40 to 120 days, but not evenly spaced. If we go from 40 to 50, we have added 25% more data, but from 110 to 120 is only 9%. The simplest way to fix this is to test 30, 45, 67, 101, and 151, which is an increase of 50% for each value. Or you can increase by 25%, as long as it's a percentage and not a fixed increment.

Define the date range for the test. With a slow trend, you'll need more data to get enough trades to consider it a valid sample. Four trades are not enough, and 100 is pretty good for a long-term trend. More is better. Be sure the data covers bull markets, bear markets, and sideways markets. That will be difficult for interest rates, which have seen yields decline, more or less, since 1980. But for stocks, going back to 1990 would cover everything you need.

What markets? That's up to you. Interest rates have the best trends but the least diversification. FX is also trending, but with shorter periods. The major currencies can show good trends, but odd crossrates may not have any. Equities are a problem. Since the financial crisis of 2008, the overall market has had a consistent trend. This also happened in the later 1990s when the dotcom companies were flying high. But it's not typical for stocks, which are normally very noisy and mean reverting. So equity index markets offer good diversification and an occasional trend, but don't count on them to be the backbone of your profitability. It's a case of "know your market."

COSTS

Don't forget to decide on the costs. We can't trade for free. A slow trend system doesn't trade often, so costs should not be a problem, but they can range from $1 to $10 per trade for equities (large orders may have a per share cost), plus there may be some slippage getting in and out. Futures can be as low as $4 or up to $15 per trade, and the slippage could be significant. Err on the side of caution, but don't burden your system with unnecessary costs.

EXPECTATIONS

Expectations are important. If we test 10 different calculation periods for the trend, how many do you expect to be profitable? Ideally, I like to see 7, or 70%. They should also be contiguous, so that if one end is a loss but all others are profitable, I deem that as successful. If profits and losses alternate, I conclude that my strategy has a random characteristic and reject it.

What about markets? If I'm testing futures, then I expect interest rates to do well—all of them. It would be suspect if U.S. Treasuries were profitable but not the Eurobund (10-year) and Eurobobl (5-year). When you add a currency into the price mix, you should expect higher volatility, but because both the interest rates and FX have strong trending components, they should all be profitable. It doesn't matter how profitable, as long as there is some consistency across the sector.

SATISFYING THE FIRST MILESTONE

It is important that the basic buy-and-sell rules are successful across a range of calculation periods and similar markets. If this fails, then you need to rethink your idea. I don't believe in adding rules to make the strategy more complex in the hope that one rule will turn a losing idea into a profitable one. It is necessary that the basic concept is robust before moving forward. Then we can try to make it better.

In Chapter 4, we looked at the results of optimizing the trend calculation period for both U.S. 30-year Treasury bonds and crude oil (see Figures 4.6 and 4.7). Both showed only one losing trend out of 60 tests, a high bar for any system. Let's skip ahead and use the euro currency, adding a stop-loss to the breakout test, where the stop is a multiple of the 20-day volatility, measured from the highest profit of the trade. It is effectively a trailing stop that doesn't retreat. Once stopped out, we can't reenter in the same direction. We need to wait for an opposite trend first. We'll guess at a reasonable stop distance of no less than 3 average true ranges (ATRs); otherwise, we'll get stopped out too often on the price noise. We choose the euro because it is generally a trending market, given the big swings in the dollar, but it has faster moves than interest rates.

A heat map of the optimization can be seen in Figure 16.1. The calculation period is the left axis, and the

Trend Period	STOP-LOSS FACTOR								
	10	9	8	7	6	5	4	3	2
100	618563	577350	454550	1715325	1707600	1178788	1464725	1547988	658838
90	611988	630875	733850	1873325	1826838	1274025	1292125	1350125	421013
80	353750	148325	34300	1298775	1063775	843975	680700	805675	−92863
70	432713	470300	537838	1411463	1280125	763525	872100	908763	−60775
60	1126100	1135900	1222425	1096275	799638	728900	373750	508138	−341500
50	998713	1005213	1022513	1058388	725888	720063	268413	552500	−432450
40	828975	828975	846275	1139738	918713	774013	450550	670013	−362675
30	777425	777425	768125	821925	765088	1290238	1203825	1046238	−28225
20	1045063	1053875	1069625	963825	977225	1006588	764375	1378075	520913

FIGURE 16.1 Optimization of the EURUSD Futures Using a Breakout and Trailing Stop

stop-loss factor is along the top. Then the slowest trend and the largest stop is in the top left corner, while the fastest trend and the closest stop is in the lower right corner. The trend results using no stop are in the right column. We show only the net profits, although you will also want to see the information ratio to help you know how much risk is associated with each return.

It is most important to see the big picture. In this case, 75 of 81 tests are profitable, making this a robust result. The only losses come at the far right, where the stop-loss is closest (a factor of 2 ATRs), meaning that it is too close and gets caught in the market noise. Using the colors on an Excel heat map, the peak profits come in the middle, indicating that our test range is good. The average gain of all 81 tests is $821,672, compared to $763,267 for the test with no stop. Overall, this specific stop-loss rule is a robust improvement for this market.

Based on this test, we would use the trailing stop, but which parameter values would we use? The best results used a 90-day breakout and a stop factor of 7. But notice that a stop factor of 8 has significantly worse results for slower trends. Is this a good choice?

There are two ways we can resolve this problem:

1. Choose multiple parameters to get a sample of the entire grid and an average return. The average return was pretty good, so that's a reasonable option.
2. Test other markets to find the best overall stop-loss factor. After all, this is a limited set of trades and we're choosing a factor that is tuned to this market. Being realistic, tuning a parameter that worked in the past doesn't mean it will work in the future. That stop could have saved the system from one very large loss, but overall would have been better had it been slightly larger.

Looking at it another way, using the average and standard deviation of the 81 test results, we can find that the best result was at the 1.3% probability level. Eek! The chance of getting another positive outcome in the future is pretty small, so multiple parameters are looking to be a more realistic choice.

Having satisfied the important step of deciding that a slow breakout strategy is robust, and that a stop-loss works for the EURUSD, we now need to look at other features.

PROFIT-TAKING

Continuing with the idea that each feature must be successful and independent of other rules, we look at the basic breakout combined with profit-taking. Using the ATR in a way similar to the stop-loss, we will measure the profit target as a factor of the ATR added or subtracted from the trade entry price. The profit target can expand or contract each day if the ATR is larger or smaller, but it is always measured from the original trade entry price, so it doesn't vary by much. In the following optimization, the breakout period is again 20 to 100 along the left, and the profit factors are 2 to 10 along the top. In Figure 16.2, the average of all tests is $766,375, compared to the average without profit-taking of $763,267, which is only a slight improvement. On the good side, the better results cluster toward the top left (larger profits and slower trend) and profit-taking gets you out of the market. It also increased the percentage of profitable trades to 68%. About ⅓ of the trades took profits, a reasonable percentage.

To get the most benefit from profit-taking, you need to be able to reset the trade at a lower price (if you were long). That allows you to capture more of an extended run. Noisier markets, such as the S&P, will benefit more from profit-taking, while the markets with the strongest trends,

Trend Period	PROFIT-TAKING FACTOR									
	10	9	8	7	6	5	4	3	2	No PT
100	630775	871337	647400	1500550	1124825	961100	579575	262612	227512	447925
90	2233288	2019713	1752750	1511838	1168575	1037013	652087	364562	315687	765375
80	2153150	1951775	1464063	1236263	881600	572425	242237	-51912	-103913	228463
70	2147700	1964913	1563025	1351438	1002863	673925	362125	75987	-18287	573775
60	1742275	1615888	1662525	1389800	1018025	658900	377900	71637	-36287	1217250
50	592425	1019913	1508175	1348525	968550	717575	473862	155762	76025	936350
40	858925	1246288	1163200	906287	372125	144412	-110825	-203788	122700	876400
30	36925	642575	600562	495562	627525	491875	333087	375912	856387	872563
20	524512	284200	265400	479675	252275	25650	-143550	89687	618187	951300

FIGURE 16.2 Breakout Optimization of EURUSD with Profit-Taking

the Eurodollar interest rates and the short Sterling, will not be improved by profit-taking.

VOLATILITY FILTER

The last rule we'll try is the volatility filter. For trending systems, entering on very high volatility, or even holding a trade when volatility is extreme, adds more risk than return—and we don't need more risk. Volatility will vary from market to market, especially in futures where there is high leverage. While the euro currency (EUR) has had some substantial swings against the U.S. dollar (USD), it has also had extended periods of very low volatility.

A volatility filter uses the annualized standard deviation of the daily price returns multiplied by the square root of 252. For most markets, an annualized volatility exceeding 0.40 (40%) is high and should be avoided. For the EURUSD, that will be much lower. We will exit any trade and not enter a new trade when the volatility is above our threshold filter.

The optimization results for the volatility filter are shown in Figure 16.3. Although the average test result is $771,117, slightly better than the benchmark of $763,267, the gains were limited to the filter size of 0.15, with the results of a smaller filter falling off considerably. We can conclude that this value is finely tuned and not robust for this market. Given the sustained low volatility, a small change in the filter size can cause a large change in performance. That won't be the case for more volatile futures markets, such as the S&P and crude oil.

Trend Period	VOLATILITY FILTER											No Vol
	0.60	0.55	0.50	0.45	0.40	0.35	0.30	0.25	0.20	0.15	0.10	
100	447925	447925	447925	447925	447925	447925	447925	447925	505725	1801900	532563	447925
90	765375	765375	765375	765375	765375	765375	765375	765375	584463	2056875	196550	765375
80	228463	228463	228463	228463	228463	228463	228463	228463	614200	1555838	312738	228463
70	573775	573775	573775	573775	573775	573775	573775	573775	623988	1732275	274700	573775
60	1217250	1217250	1217250	1217250	1217250	1217250	1217250	1217250	265725	1428850	28375	1217250
50	936350	936350	936350	936350	936350	936350	936350	936350	385925	1584138	-31250	936350
40	876400	876400	876400	876400	876400	876400	876400	876400	1012400	1151488	-394075	876400
30	872563	872563	872563	872563	872563	872563	872563	872563	902663	833863	99163	872563
20	951300	951300	951300	951300	951300	951300	951300	951300	998038	1388550	939738	951300

FIGURE 16.3 Optimization of EURUSD Futures with a Breakout and Volatility Filter

COMBINING RULES

Let's say that we're happy with the breakout approach, the stop-loss, and profit-taking for the EURUSD. We'll put the volatility filter aside for now because the results were not as robust as we wanted.

If you select the best calculation period, the best stop-loss, and the best profit threshold, you've created a badly overfitted system. It may work, but it's unlikely to come anywhere close to expectations unless the future price movement is just the same as the past.

Instead, we need to set our goal as the average return of a group of tests. In this case, we can use the average optimization result. For example, if we consider the breakout with no options, the best result was a gain of $1,217,250, using the 60-day breakout. On the other hand, the average of all tests from 20 to 100 days was $763,267, about 37% lower. Realistically, we don't know what will happen in the future, and we don't know which calculation period will be best, so the average is our best guess. That should be your expectation.

MULTIPLE ENTRIES AND EXITS

The same is true of each rule added to your system. Of course, it's easier to test a single profit target or stop-loss threshold. But for the trend itself, and for profit-taking, it's not best to use only one parameter value. Putting your entire trade on a single signal can get you the best result or worst result, the same as trading only one stock. Diversification into more than one stock, given that you expect them all to do well, will result in an average return but often a much lower risk, depending on how closely correlated they are. The average return is realistic.

If you're a risk taker, then one trend speed and one profit target is what you want, but I prefer a little less excitement, so I opt for multiple parameters wherever possible. To be practical, we won't trade all the breakout periods or all the profit targets. We can use three breakout calculation periods and three profit targets, in each case trading ⅓ of the total position. We should come close to getting the average.

As a system developer, you need to perform all these steps yourself, and combine them into a single system. However, there is one more important step.

MORE MARKETS, MORE ROBUSTNESS

While we've successfully found parameters for the EURUSD trend strategy, and choosing three calculation periods and other multiple parameters moves us away from overfitting, it is not enough. Some researchers accept the idea that each market may have a different set of parameters, and a different volatility factor for stops and profit-taking, because each market, or stock, has a unique pattern.

I'm not in that group. I believe that testing using more data is safer and brings you to a more generalized conclusion. If you also believe that, then you test a larger set of unrelated markets and find the parameters that work best across all the markets. That's done by running the same optimization test and averaging the results that show in the corresponding boxes.

It may turn out that the average result over many markets doesn't look as good as the average result for a single stock or futures market. But the average result gained from using the same parameter applied to multiple markets will give you an even better idea of what to expect.

The other way of thinking is that using different parameters for different markets is another way of getting diversification. It's a valid argument, but it's a philosophical difference. Using the same parameters forces you to generalize the rules, our "loose pants" solution. I can't tell you which is best, only that I prefer the same parameters, at least for all futures market or stocks in the same sector.

STABILIZING THE RISK

Risk control must be everywhere in your trading system. The two most important places are at the very start of each trade and when all of your markets are combined into a portfolio. We've discussed these issues in Chapter 14.

The risk for each trade should be the same. By doing that, you maximize your diversification. For stocks, you simply allocate an equal dollar amount to each trade and divide by the current price. For futures, you calculate the dollar value of the 20-day ATR and divide that into the same investment size for each market. The process is called *volatility parity*.

Even with equal risk, the volatility of all markets fluctuates, sometimes in the extreme. You'll need to decide your risk tolerance. You measure the volatility using the annualized volatility formula applied to the daily portfolio returns. For most investors, something under 12% is comfortable.

For equities, you can only deleverage when the volatility is too high because adding volatility means buying more shares, which in turn requires a larger investment. It's a circle that never ends. For futures trading, which normally has large reserves, you can scale up or down by changing your position size equally across your holdings. The objective is to increase leverage when the market is quiet and often producing profits, and decrease when there is too much risk, whether or not there are profits. We want to avoid risk because what is good today can be ugly tomorrow.

DO IT YOURSELF

There have been a lot of little steps left out of this example for the sake of simplicity. As you develop strategies yourself and construct portfolios, you'll need to rethink the entire process until you're comfortable with it. There is no need to rush. The market will wait for you. This example was to give you an outline to follow, and a review of the most important points. If I gave more than that, I would be creating the system for you, which is contrary to the principle of "teach a man to fish."

CHAPTER 17

Constructing an Intraday Trading Strategy

I strongly suggest that you read the previous chapter, Constructing a Trend Strategy, because it contains a lot of material that won't be repeated here. The process for developing a trading strategy has many common elements of which the underlying trading rules may turn out to be the smallest part.

The major concept that differentiates intraday trading from long-term trend following is clearly the high frequency data, for example 5-minute or 15-minute bars instead of daily or weekly prices. That changes the focus of the strategy away from economic trends to market noise, repeated patterns, and the behavior of traders. It becomes you against them.

Trading costs and execution timing also become important. When your trade has a short holding period, the costs become a significant obstacle. You can no longer place your order "at the market," but must use limit orders and try to beat the system entry and exit prices. It's not something you can do part-time, and it may not work for orders that are automatically sent for execution unless you are very sophisticated.

Let's assume we're not going to compete with the high frequency traders; instead, we'll find a slightly longer time frame that can produce a larger return per share or per contract. In this venue, individual market characteristics will surface. In some cases, equities and futures markets will have a high degree of noise—erratic movements—which will lend itself to mean reversion. Other markets, such as Apple, Netflix, Eurodollar interest rates, and the euro currency, will exhibit more trends and you'll want to take advantage of that direction. Distinguishing which market goes with which strategy will be an important part of successful trading, and moreso for short-term trading.

THE TIME FRAME

The first step is deciding the time frame, the bar size in minutes, in which you'll operate. The shorter the time bar, the smaller the profits and losses. The shorter the time bar, the more likely you'll see increased noise and you'll want to apply mean reversion instead of a directional approach.

For practical purposes, we'll use 20- and 30-minute bars, but we know the high and low of those bars, so we can anticipate a profit target or stop-loss, provided two events don't occur on the same bar. We'll stay with futures markets, but for this example we'll use the emini S&P, the most popular contract and one with a lot of price noise.

OUTLINE

The process of developing an intraday strategy is essentially the same as the trend method, with perhaps an extra step distinguishing which markets require mean reversion instead of a trend preference. Some of the unique decisions to be made are:

- Size of price bars in minutes.
- Trending quality of the market to decide on mean reversion, directional trading, or a combination.
- Do you hold the trade overnight or is it simply a day trade?
- Should you enter after a specific time or on the close?
- Is there a maximum volatility?
- Are results better when they are preceded by an inside day?
- Should you take trades only in the direction of the daily or longer-term trend?

We also have the position sizing, profit-taking, stop-losses, and other risk controls similar to the previous example of a trend strategy to consider. Those are a lot of options to test, so we'll need to reason out some of them to pare down the process.

For example, do we want to filter trades using the direction of the trend? If this is the only strategy you're trading, then yes, because the trend can add reliability and increase the size of your profits. But if you have multiple strategies, then using a trend will make the performance of even an intraday system show high correlations to other trend systems. For that reason, we won't show test results using the trend as an option.

We'll also choose to hold a trade overnight in order to increase the chances of a larger profit. Then we won't need to decide on the last time of day to enter a trade because we should be allowed to enter on the close. You may still want to know what time of day to stop entering orders because getting a signal on the close may be difficult to execute, except in the aftermarket. Getting the last signal 15 minutes before the close may be more practical.

DECIDING ON THE STRATEGY

There are two popular strategies for intraday trading:

1. A breakout from an early trading range.
2. A move in excess of some threshold measured from the close of the previous day.

Either one could be directional (trending) or mean reverting.

CHOOSING A STRATEGY

We're not going to test all the possible strategies here, because that would take away the fun that you'll have developing your own. Showing too much detail will also cause you to favor my solutions when you should be putting your own personality into your trading system. That way you are most likely to follow it through good and bad times.

A breakout of an opening range (say, the first hour of trading) or a move measured from the opening price, has the advantage of being independent of the previous day and not related to the trend of prices. On the other hand, it means getting into the trade later and makes a day trade much more difficult. Our choice will then be to buy an upward breakout, or sell a downward breakout, based on the previous close and daily volatility. We will apply it to the *e*mini S&P futures, which should also work on the sector SPDR ETF, the SPY.

Note that we'll use the daily volatility, not intraday. Experience has shown that intraday volatility has a pattern that is lower in the middle of the day. That results in a breakout signal shortly afterward when the market normally becomes more active. We don't really want to get a trading signal every day at 1 P.M. just because the traders have come back from lunch.

DIRECTIONAL OR MEAN REVERTING

A volatility breakout system is traditionally a directional trade. The market opens, it flounders for a while, and then picks a direction. If prices open sharply higher or lower relative to the previous close, it's likely to be a good opportunity for a mean reverting trade, exiting quickly on a small profit but no later than the close of the day. Because of the need for an extreme opening, there are fewer opportunities and higher risk than trading in the price direction. Returns are also smaller because the trade isn't held as long. You may want to allow trading signals based price moves relative to both today's open and the previous close, just to increase your opportunities.

A directional trade has the advantages of being able to stay with the trade overnight. In some way, it has its own very short-term trend. You hold the trade until you reach your profit target or until the next day generates a signal in the opposite direction.

This method can generate a lot of trades if the breakout criterion is small. That allows you to filter those trades with rules such as:

- Minimum or maximum volatility.
- Preceded by an inside day or by compression (a series of lower volatility days).
- Various charting patterns, such as hooks.

We will look at volatility in our process to find a good strategy, but the patterns will be left for you to develop on your own.

THE BASIC RULES

The basic rules for the volatility breakout have been around for a long time, but there are better and worse ways to implement them. We will limit our tests to just a few features to give you a better idea of the process.

We will also assume that each trade has equal risk to avoid any bias, as discussed in the previous chapter, and we will use data that includes 2008 to be sure the system can survive extreme risk.

THE BREAKOUT RULE

We tested both the breakout based on today's open and one based on the previous close. We bought or sold in the direction of the breakout. The previous close won hands down. Using the previous close means that any gap opening is likely to generate a trading signal.

Volatility was based on the daily average true range, so the first test plotted the volatility period against the volatility breakout factor, measured from the previous close. The trade was held until there was a new trading signal, not the best rule, but the simplest. Figure 17.1 shows the results of the SP mini from 2005.

Compared to the trend system in the previous chapter, this is not a robust result. Nevertheless, we can understand it. The volatility calculation period is not as important as the breakout factor, because the results in each column are generally similar, that is, most are either profits or losses.

When the breakout is very small, below 0.50, the signal is unreliable, generating consistent losses. When the breakout is very large, it must enter just when prices have

INTRADAY BREAKOUT FACTOR

Vol Period	1.500	1.375	1.250	1.125	1.000	0.875	0.750	0.625	0.500	0.375	0.250
30	−18450	−14161	16875	−37193	−17513	9997	50146	52555	20819	−9382	−56637
25	−41357	−30175	−34371	−29716	−9871	8108	32597	41530	18996	−18247	−53997
20	−84643	−54633	−48237	−27538	−2842	13501	28363	21466	40248	−18555	−54612
15	−80834	−72164	−67856	−72077	−7035	10297	21432	−1523	25083	−15187	−57823
10	−45312	−65622	−95757	−61985	−27190	−13749	41390	5697	20236	−19338	−57596
5	−21637	−48639	−67444	−65935	−21249	−9069	21474	10406	3360	−16045	−58397

FIGURE 17.1 Optimization of emini SP Futures from 2005, Volatility Period versus Intraday Breakout Factor

reached their extremes, also producing a loss or reducing potential profits. The losses associated with the large breakout factors could be considered good news, because we can easily sell an upward breakout using a mean reversion rule and turn the loss into a profit.

The best duster came when the breakout factor was from 0.75 to 0.50 and the volatility period was at least 20. The best result was a period of 30 and a breakout factor of 0.625.

PROFIT TAKING AND EXTREME VOLATILITY

We'll look at two of the more important add-ons, profit-taking and extreme volatility. Profit-taking is important because we don't expect prices to continue in the direction of the breakout for very long, remembering that there is too much noise in high frequency data.

Using the best parameters from the previous test (yes, that's overfitting, but it's only an example), we compare the results against the previous profit of $52,625 (see Figure 17.2). Overall, the results are worse, but larger

Max $Vol	PROFIT-TAKING FACTOR								
	2.00	1.75	1.50	1.25	1.00	0.75	0.50	0.25	0.00
2,000	53286	53668	67841	71295	59293	49886	45616	41266	44024
1,750	51052	51809	66282	70111	58459	49427	44712	40357	45365
1,500	54298	55305	69707	70873	58196	48930	44448	37870	54411
1,250	34094	37351	39736	34725	34897	25765	26339	20867	43985
1,000	6890	8512	12497	11563	4605	6051	2366	4231	-10008
750	8962	7283	11714	5585	10511	3990	50	291	34354
500	10722	11942	10643	8053	6667	5305	5397	4844	-5583

FIGURE 17.2 Intraday Breakout Optimization of the emini SP Varying the Maximum Volatility in Dollars and the Profit-Taking Factor

volatility and a profit factor above 1.0 are better. Because the returns get better as the volatility threshold increases, we will conclude that a maximum volatility limit doesn't work and that profit-taking with a factor of 1.25 is the best choice.

By way of explanation, profit-taking is important because it gets you out of the market. If you can get the same returns by being in the market less time, you can avoid unnecessary risk. It is not necessary to always improve the returns. Less exposure is equally as good.

WHAT ABOUT THE TREND?

It seems reasonable that trading in the direction of the trend could increase returns considerably. Knowing that the stock market, not just the U.S. market, but nearly all world equity markets, are biased to the upside would seem to support that opinion. If we take the best results that we have so far, filter it with a trend, and take only the long trades, life should be good.

It turns out not to be quite so obvious. In Figure 17.3, we show the trend calculation period along the bottom (number of days), and the net profit along the left for both long-short trades and long only. We expected that the long-only will be better because of the upward bias, and that turns out to be true. However, neither is as good as not using the trend, as seen at the far right. But that may not be the full answer. A trend filter will keep you out of the market when the trend direction conflicts with the signal direction. Being out of the market can be good and the way to decide the benefit is to compare the information ratios

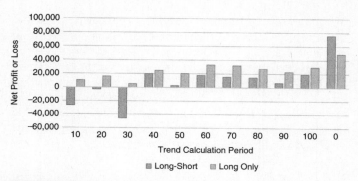

FIGURE 17.3 Results from Testing the Trend as a Filter

of the two approaches. A higher ratio means a better return for the risk. But on an absolute basis, returns will be lower.

When we put it all together, using a daily volatility period of 30, a breakout of 0.625, profit-taking of 1.25, and allow the trades to be held overnight, we get the profits shown in Figure 17.4. Trading both longs and shorts nets a higher return, but trading longs only is smoother. It's your choice.

The last figure, 17.5, shows the actual trading signals on a TradeStation chart. *BOup* means a buy signal generated by a breakout to the upside. *PTlong* and *PTshort* means that the profit targets were reached for a long or short sale. Be reminded that this was a short example and did not explore many features and did not look for robustness over a wide range of markets.

Because of the higher frequency data, variations in the personalities of markets will become more important. Those markets with lower volume may be significantly less

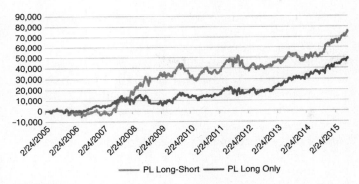

FIGURE 17.4   Results Using the Final Intraday Breakout Parameters

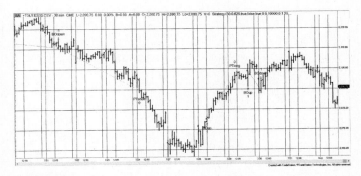

FIGURE 17.5   Example of Trading Signals for the Intraday
Breakout Applied to 30-Minute *e*Mini S&P Prices

predictable, or they may present a mean reverting opportunity for small position sizes.

We didn't use any stop-loss orders in any of these examples, but risk control is important. One approach is to ask if the trade is profitable at the end of the day, or at some specific time. Most floor traders like their positions to show a profit very early, but using profits to decide whether to hold the trade overnight seems to be one good way to control risk while giving the trade some time to develop.

As you develop systems on your own, you will think of many more options and different ways to qualify the markets. Success is always achieved by hard work.

CHAPTER **18**

Summary

I stated in the Introduction that this book is short so that you would read it all. I've tried to limit each section to only those ideas that every algorithmic trader will need to confront and resolve in order to be successful. I'm sure there are other important concepts that I've omitted.

The following is a brief summary of those items that I don't think you should forget:

1. Your strategy must have a sound premise.
2. Your strategy must match your trading personality.
3. Fewer rules and clear ideas are most likely to be successful.
4. Each rule must stand on its own as successful.
5. The best strategies work in many markets and over a sufficient number of years.
6. When volatility is very high, the risk is not worth the reward.
7. Use multiple parameters to stabilize your results.
8. Use stops only to protect against disasters. Try to use your strategy's natural exit.
9. Take profits if you're a short-term trader, but not if you're a trend follower. Use multiple target levels.

10. There is no perfect system. Accept and manage the risk. You can always trade smaller positions.
11. Accept when your system didn't work on out-of-sample data and move on. Don't try to remove an individual loss.
12. When you're out of the market, you can't suffer a price shock.
13. When ranking stocks for your portfolio, simple is better.
14. Use equal-weighting wherever possible.
15. Strategy diversification is better than market diversification.

One last point: It's good to listen to and read about other strategies. Some of them will appeal to you. Be careful, because they tend to use only good examples, and the strategy may not work on a broad set of markets or over many years. You must test it yourself to know its true value. That goes for many of the techniques that I have shared in this short book. It's your money. Invest it wisely.

Good Trading!

Resources

The following websites provide trading development platforms, blogs about trading techniques, and general financial information that may stimulate trading ideas. The User Groups can be very helpful at all levels of development.

SYSTEM DEVELOPMENT PLATFORMS

AbleTrend	www.ablesys.com
AIQ	www.aiqsystems.com
AmiBroker	www.amibroker.com
eSignal, Advanced GET	www.esignal.com
MetaStock (Pro)	www.metastock.com
Microsoft Excel (Visual Basic)	www.microsoft.com
MultiCharts	www.multicharts.com
NeuroShell Trader Professional	www.neuroshell.com
NinjaTrader	www.ninjatrader.com
OmniTrader	www.omnitrader.com
TradersStudio (Turbo)	www.tradersstudio.com

TradeStation	www.TradeStation.com
Updata	www.updata.co.uk
VisualTrader	www.omnitrader.com
VectorVest 7 EOD	www.vectorvest.com
Wealth-Lab (Pro)	www.wealth-lab.com

User Groups:

MetaStock (see website under System Development Platforms)

UsingEasyLanguage.com

BLOGS

More technical trading:

http://ibankcoin.com/

http://investorsinsight.com

http://liquidalpha.blogspot.com

http://marketsci.wordpress.com/

http://peterlbrandt.com/

http://quantifiableedges.blogspot.com/

http://vixandmore.blogspot.com/

More scientific:

www.epchan.blogspot.com

www.quantivity.wordpress.com/

www.onlyvix.blogspot.com/
www.cxoadvisory.com/blog/

Scholarly research:
www.ssrn.com/

Financial Blogs:
AbnormalReturns.com
Clusterstock.tumblr.com
CrossingWallStreet.com
CSSAnalytics.wordpress.com
Dr. Ed's Blog (blog.yardeni.com)
InsiderMonkey.com
johnhcochrane.blogspot.com
SeekingAlpha.com
StreetSleuth.com
Rithholtz.com (The Big Picture)
World Beta (MebFaber.com)

PERIODICALS

Modern Trader
Technical Analysis of Stocks & Commodities
Traders-Mag

MTA Technically Speaking
Journal of Futures Markets
Journal of Portfolio Management

PERRY KAUFMAN WEBSITES

www.Perrykaufman.com
www.KaufmanSignals.com
www.KaufmanAnalytics.com

Index